ourplace

suzy chiazzari

ourplace

suzy chiazzari

WATSON-GUPTILL PUBLICATONS
NEW YORK

First published in the United States in 2002 by
Watson-Guptill Publications
a division of VNU Business Media, Inc.
770 Broadway, New York, New York 10003
www.watsonguptill.com

Conceived and created by
Axis Publishing Limited
8c Accommodation Road
London NW11 8ED
www.axispublishing.co.uk

Creative Director: Siân Keogh
Managing Editor: Matthew Harvey
Project Designers: Juliet Brown, Anna Knight
Project Editor: Kim Davies
Production Manager: Sue Bayliss
Photographer: Mike Good
Illustrators: Sebastian Quigley and John Woodcock

Text and images copyright
© Axis Publishing Limited 2002

Note
The opinions and advice expressed in this book are
intended as a guide only. The publisher and author
accept no responsibility for any injury or loss
sustained as a result of using this book.

1 2 3 4 5 6 / 07 06 05 04 03 02

Library of Congress Control Number: 2002100037

ISBN: 0–8230–0374–4

Separation by United Graphic Pte Limited
Printed and bound in China by Toppan Printing

contents

ENTRANCE HALL
LIVING ROOM
KITCHEN
BEDROOM
BATHROOM

DISCUSSION
FOCUS
INSPIRATION
INTERACTION

how to use this book

THIS BOOK HAS BEEN DESIGNED TO HELP YOU ENHANCE YOUR HOME AND SO ENHANCE YOUR RELATIONSHIPS. EACH CHAPTER FOCUSES ON ONE AREA OF THE HOME, AND GUIDES YOU THROUGH FOUR DISTINCT STAGES: DISCUSSION, FOCUS, INSPIRATION, AND INTERACTION. FOLLOWING THE PROCESS FOR EACH AREA WILL HELP YOU CHANGE YOUR HOME FOR THE BETTER.

DISCUSSION   The Discussion pages take a general look at the area or room in question. They prompt you to examine the way that you use the area and show how to spot signs of relationship problems. Discussion pages also explain the special role that particular areas play in our emotions and the impact that improvements can have on our lives.

FOCUS   Focus pages highlight particular issues that can arise in each area of the home. They help you look objectively at the impact that these issues have on relationships, using questionnaires to help you examine exactly how a problem affects you.

INSPIRATION   These pages provide a range of different approaches to using your home spaces. Each one looks at the elements that make up a well-designed room, and provides tips on how to achieve a stunning result.

INTERACTION   Once you have come up with some ideas on how you would like to change an area of your home, you need a plan. The Interaction pages help you come up with a plan that includes everyone's needs—from your partner to your cat. They use questionnaires to help you resolve particular issues and provide tips on some possible changes. They encourage positive interaction as a way of improving your home—and your relationships.

introduction

IN THIS CHAPTER YOU CAN EXPLORE THE CONNECTION BETWEEN YOU, YOUR HOME, AND YOUR RELATIONSHIPS. OUR HOMES ARE MUCH MORE THAN JUST BRICKS AND MORTAR, THEY ARE THE NEST THAT NURTURES OUR PHYSICAL, EMOTIONAL, AND SPIRITUAL GROWTH. INNER HEALTH IS REFLECTED IN THE STATE OF THE HOME—JUST AS THE STATE OF THE HOME CAN INFLUENCE INNER WELL-BEING. BEFORE LOOKING AT EACH AREA OF YOUR PLACE IN DETAIL LATER IN THE BOOK, IT IS WORTH LOOKING AT SOME OF THE FUNDAMENTAL WAYS THAT YOUR HOME CAN AFFECT YOU AND SOME OF THE WARNING SIGNS IT CAN GIVE YOU ABOUT YOUR INNER HEALTH AND YOUR RELATIONSHIPS.

our homes, ourselves

OUR HOME IS A SPECIAL PLACE WHERE WE CAN RELAX AND LET GO OF THE PRESSURES OF THE OUTSIDE WORLD. IT IS HERE THAT WE DISPLAY OUR TRUE SELVES. IN OUR OWN PERSONAL SPACE, WE ARE FREE TO EXPRESS OUR PERSONALITY, OUR VALUES, AND OUR LIFESTYLE; AND THIS HAS A GREAT IMPACT ON OUR LIVING ENVIRONMENT. YOUR HOME REFLECTS THE INNER YOU AND THE WAY YOU SEE THE WORLD.

It is commonly accepted that the outer world reflects the inner world of thoughts and feelings. Our physical home environment reflects what psychologists call our "inner house." Our choice of home, its contents and decoration, as well as the way in which we look after it, all reveal different things about ourselves.

our homes and our relationships

Throughout our lives we are involved in relationships, both with our environment and with each other. These relationships can be good or bad, happy or sad. Some are transitory, while others last a lifetime.

Most of us spend more than 90 percent of our lives indoors, and it is in the home that our most significant relationships unfold and come to life. While our home is a statement of who we are, it is also a means of communicating our thoughts and feelings to others. A relationship with a live-in partner is often strongly mirrored in the home. Not only does your home reflect your personal state of mind, it can also mirror the way you see yourselves as a couple and what you want from your relationship. A healthy, balanced home contains elements that reflect the character and tastes of all who live in it.

The idea that your home reflects your life also holds true when more than two people share the space. Shared homes can clearly reveal the way that people in the home inter-

COUPLES

The state and appearance of your home will tell you a lot about your relationship. The process of examining the home with an open mind will also shine a spotlight onto your relationship. This will help you to make beneficial changes to your home that will reflect and enhance positive changes in the way you relate and communicate with each other.

FAMILIES

The home is the castle of the family, providing a safe and nurturing environment that meets the needs of you as an individual, you as a parent, and you as a family. Taking a fresh look at the home from a relationship point of view will help you to increase harmony within the family group and make sure that each individual is reflected and acknowledged in the home.

act with one another and the state of their relationships. By understanding the messages that your home can hold, you can come to understand and improve your relationships with yourself, your partner, family and friends, or whoever you share your home with.

what your home says about you

Imagine that you are strangers visiting your home for the first time. Walk around your place, starting at the front door and visiting every room in the house. As you do this, look around you and think about the impressions you get with regards to the type of people who live there. The style, colors, furnishings,

WHAT YOUR HOME SAYS TO YOU ABOUT YOU

ON A SCALE OF ONE TO TEN, HOW STRONG IS YOUR IMPRESSION THAT THE PEOPLE LIVING IN THE HOME ARE:	person A	person B	person C	person D
houseproud				
friendly				
caring				
unconventional				
messy slobs				
have traditional values				
perfectionists				
intimidating				
withdrawn				
family-oriented				

(ADD ANY OTHER CHARACTERISTICS THAT CAME TO MIND AS YOU WALKED AROUND YOUR HOME AND RATE THEM ON A SCALE OF ONE TO TEN AS WELL.)

HOMESHARERS

When casual acquaintances share a home, it is in many ways more crucial than ever that relationships are taken into account within the home. Different backgrounds and personalities can be harmonized if the right steps are taken.

EXTENDED FAMILIES

Extending a family home to embrace senior family members or relations can cause stressful changes in the energy within the home. By dealing with changes in an open and thoughtful way, there is no reason why harmony cannot be achieved.

and atmosphere will give you clues about the personality and interests of the occupants. The state of the house—whether it is well-maintained, messy, or neat—will also help you form an opinion about the general attitude of the people who live there. Afterward, look at the list above and give your home marks from one to ten depending on how strong an impression you get. It's a good idea to write down your marks individually, then compare them with those of your partner or homesharers. Now, discuss!

where you live

HOW YOU FEEL ABOUT YOUR HOME AND NEIGHBORHOOD DEPENDS ON YOUR EXPECTATIONS OF IT AND HOW CLOSELY IT LIVES UP TO THEM. LEARNING TO ACCEPT A HOME THAT IS NOT PERFECT IS LIKE LEARNING TO LIVE WITH ANOTHER PERSON. YOU HAVE TO ACCEPT HIS OR HER GOOD AND BAD TRAITS, AND CREATE A SPACE WHERE YOU CAN BOTH FEEL GOOD WITHOUT COMPROMISING EACH OTHER.

Your neighborhood

Like your home, the neighborhood you live in says something about your lifestyle, status, and the way you see yourself or wish others to see you. When people have a change of circumstances, it is not unusual for them to want to move home to somewhere more in keeping with their new image.

Being surrounded by people and places that are familiar to us makes us feel comfortable and gives us a sense of belonging. Many people enjoy living close to their place of birth or the area where they spent their childhood. However, today's couples are much less likely to come from the same place, and one or both partners are likely to have to move away from their comfort zone. Creating a new place that provides you with home comforts and addresses your needs is therefore all the more important if you are to enjoy a lasting relationship with a partner—or co-exist peacefully with others sharing your home. With your homesharers, try to come up with two or three words that you think

MY MAIN INTENTION FOR MY HOME IS:	person A	PERSON B	PERSON C	PERSON D
to start my life afresh.				
to put down roots.				
to live near my family or in-laws.				
to give me a project or indulge an interest/ hobby.				
to allow my relationship to develop and mature.				
to start a family.				
to bring up my children.				
to allow me to live near my work.				
to enjoy my retirement.				
other				

ALTHOUGH YOU AND YOUR PARTNER MAY HAVE DIFFERENT INTENTIONS, YOU CAN LINK THEM INTO A COMMON VISION. KEEPING YOUR INTENTION IN MIND WHEN YOU FURNISH YOUR HOME WILL HELP YOU TO PLAN AND DECORATE YOUR PLACE IN AN APPROPRIATE MANNER.

NAMING YOUR PLACE

GIVING YOUR HOME A NAME, AS HAPPENS IN MANY COUNTRIES, CAN SIGNAL YOUR INTENTION FOR THAT HOME. HOUSE NAMES LIKE FISHERMAN'S DEN OR HAPPY RETREAT GIVE AWAY THE OWNERS' INTENTIONS FOR THEIR HOME. DOES YOUR HOME HAVE A NAME? IF NOT, DECIDE ON ONE WITH YOUR PARTNER. YOU DON'T HAVE TO DISPLAY THE NAME, BUT THINKING ONE UP CAN BE AN INTERESTING EXERCISE.

HOW TO NAME YOUR HOME

WHEN CHOOSING A NAME, YOU SHOULD THINK ABOUT THE UNIQUE AND ATTRACTIVE FEATURES OF YOUR HOME AND ITS LOCATION. YOU CAN ALSO BLESS YOUR PLACE BY CREATING A SYMBOLIC NAME THAT HAS THE QUALITIES YOU WISH TO INSTILL INTO YOUR HOME. HERE ARE THREE WAYS TO HELP YOU CHOOSE A SPECIAL HOUSE NAME.

Choose a name that incorporates something of interest in the landscape around you—a special tree, or view perhaps of a mountain, the ocean, or a river.

Choose a name that relates to the people in your place—your name, a personal hobby, or your intention for being there.

Choose a name that reflects the special qualities you would like to bring into your home. These qualities could be represented by your favorite animal, plant, or flower.

sum up your neighborhood. Is it a trendy area filled with sophisticated loft dwellers, for example, or a traditional rural place that suits the country life? How comfortable do you feel with where you are living?

your intention for your home

Homes have a natural life span. You may be resident for just a few weeks, or you may spend the rest of your life within those walls. To a large extent, the length of time you spend there and the amount of effort you are willing to put into your home will depend on the intention that you have for it. This intention is often tied up with the unconscious decision that lay behind your choice of home. Understanding your intentions and those of your partner or other homesharers will help you to create a home environment that will satisfy your expectations and give you emotional security.

SEE ALSO

ENTRANCES AND HALLWAYS   PAGE 32

FRONT DOORS   PAGE 34

THE GENTLE WELCOME   PAGE 46

GETTING STARTED   PAGE 138

the healthy home

IF YOU ARE TO ENJOY A POSITIVE OUTLOOK AND HEALTHY RELATIONSHIPS, YOU NEED TO MAKE SURE YOUR HOME IS HEALTHY, TOO. JUST AS WE NEED TO EAT WHOLESOME NOURISHING FOOD IF WE ARE TO STAY HEALTHY, WE ALSO NEED TO LIVE IN A HEALTHY HOME FILLED WITH NATURAL LIGHT AND FRESH AIR. WE ALSO NEED EMOTIONAL NOURISHMENT, AND THIS WE CAN FIND IN THE ATMOSPHERE OR ENERGY OF OUR HOME. A LOVING HOME IS VERY SUPPORTIVE, ESPECIALLY IN TIMES OF STRESS.

Your home can affect you on all levels, from the physical to the emotional and mental, as well as impacting on your relationships. First and foremost, the quality and amount of natural light and fresh air in your home can have a huge effect on your energy levels, sleep, sexual behavior, and ability to deal with stress. Sunlight is the world's most important source of natural energy. It affects our physical and mental well-being on a daily basis, and it is also a source of chi, or life energy (see page 17). Therefore, it is essential that you maximize the amount of natural light entering your home, especially in winter.

Your home can be a huge asset in creating a positive and healthy mental attitude. A clean, neat, and organized home can free you from muddled thinking and help you focus on

points to remember:

■ Light, air, furniture, and room layouts affect your physical health.

■ The style of your home and your personal objects affect your personal image.

■ Colors, lighting,, and aromas affect your mood and emotions.

■ Organization, storage and home management affect your mental health.

■ The subtle atmosphere in your home supports your spiritual health.

the important things in life, while a messy and uncared-for home will make it more difficult for you to maintain mental clarity. The concept of a healthy home is one that supports and nurtures you and your relationships, rather than one that your relationship has to be strong enough to survive.

Our emotional state is strongly affected by the lighting, aroma, and colors around us, which reflect back a kaleidoscope of feelings and emotions. By introducing inspirational colors, sounds, scents, and lighting into your home, you can change and enhance your moods as well as promote positive interactions within the home. A healthy and harmonious home should have a good balance of lighting tones, scents, and sounds.

ALARM SIGNALS IN THE HOME

WHILE YOUR HOME CAN HAVE A POSITIVE EFFECT ON YOUR HEALTH, IT CAN ALSO ACT AS AN ALARM CALL, LETTING YOU KNOW THAT YOU NEED TO TAKE STEPS TO RESTORE HARMONY. NEGLECT, OUT-OF-DATE DECOR, AND ACCUMULATING MESS CAN ALL BE SIGNS THAT YOUR RELATIONSHIP NEEDS ATTENTION. LOOK AROUND AND SEE WHETHER ANY OF THE FOLLOWING ALARM SIGNALS APPLY IN YOUR HOME.

symptoms	what they mean
a dirty, permanently cluttered home	messy relationships with no boundaries
dark, dreary colors and furnishings	disillusionment and fading relationship
a stuffy atmosphere	people who are tired or bored with each other
lots of dark or heavy furniture	no room to move, a feeling of being trapped
your living room is taken over by one person's belongings and taste	an unequal partnership
very minimal style	tight controls on your relationship
one person does all the chores	disrespect, adult/child relationship
uncomfortable or sparse furniture	formal, uncomfortable relationship
no dining area	lack of communication, cohesion, or closeness
small uncomfortable bed or single beds	stressful relationship, poor sex life
no travel souvenirs or photos of you as a couple	a new or casual relationship
unfinished decoration project	problem with commitment, decision making

IF YOU HAVE DISCOVERED ANY OF THESE ALARM SIGNALS IN YOUR PLACE, DON'T WORRY. THIS BOOK IS INTENDED TO HELP YOU IMPROVE YOUR HOME AND YOUR RELATIONSHIP AT THE SAME TIME. AS A STARTING POINT, YOU MAY FIND IT HELPFUL TO DISCUSS ANY ALARM SIGNALS YOU NOTICE WITH YOUR PARTNER OR HOMESHARERS AND TALK THROUGH WHAT THEY REFLECT ABOUT YOUR RELATIONSHIP. SPOTTING ALARM SIGNALS IS A POSITIVE STEP TOWARD A HEALTHY HOME.

Self-image is an important factor in the way we interact with other people. If our home reflects our true identity, it helps us to feel confident and maintain good self-esteem. The decorating style, furniture, furnishings, and colors we choose can all help support our self-image and make us feel good about ourselves and comfortable with others. If we are comfortable with our homes, we are comfortable with ourselves.

SEE ALSO

CHOOSING COLOR PAGE 22

LIGHT AND COLOR PAGE 150

AROMATHERAPY PAGE 152

SOUND THERAPY PAGE 154

how different rooms impact on relationships

YOUR HOME IS NOT JUST AN ARRANGEMENT OF BUILDING MATERIALS. IT IS A LIVING, BREATHING ENTITY THAT TAKES IN NOURISHMENT FROM THE ENERGETIC FORCES THAT FLOW THROUGH THE UNIVERSE. LIKE A BODY, IT IS MADE UP OF DIFFERENT PARTS THAT ALL NEED TO FUNCTION WELL AND IN HARMONY WITH EACH OTHER FOR THE WHOLE TO BE HEALTHY AND EFFECTIVE.

When there is love in your life, the home becomes alive and powerful—filled with positive energy or chi. Life-giving energy flows through the power centers of the home, which in turn affect our physical health as well as our emotional and mental state. The type of energy circulating through your home will influence your health and mood. This will in turn have an effect on your relationships within your home.

We use different areas of the home for different purposes, so, not surprisingly, each area or room nourishes and supports different areas of our life. Each room carries its own particular elemental energy, which relates to a corresponding part of life. The colors, scents, furniture, and furnishings all give off their own vibrations. All of these resonances have an impact on your energy and mood, and affect the way you relate to others.

ENTRANCES

The doors and entranceways are your home's eyes and mouth, and through them you and your home connect to the outside world. It is through our front door that we invite people into our home and through the windows that we permit nourishing light, air, and life-giving chi to circulate inside. Earth energy is strong in the entrance hall, for it is in this space that you become grounded. Here the earth connection helps you touch base—you become tuned to the atmosphere in your home.

THE LIVING ROOM

The living room is the center of many homes, providing you with the opportunity to express who you really are. Your living room reflects your individual personality, tastes, and lifestyle, and you can draw on the powerful energy in this room to give you self-confidence and build self-esteem. The element of fire is strong in the living room, and this life-giving energy can be centered around the hearth and fireplace. Fire is a dynamic and creative element, full of surprises and constantly changing. The fire element in this room can refresh and enliven your relationships and stimulate creativity.

THE BEDROOM

The bedroom is a private space where you can unwind, be intimate with a partner, and renew your energy through sleep. The fire element that flows through the bedroom imbues it with regenerative and creative qualities. The attention you give your bedroom and the amount of time your spend there will reflect your ability to care for yourself, as well as the level of intimacy in your relationships.

meeting your needs

Different rooms are linked to different aspects of your health, the state of your relationships, and health of your home. Decide which aspect of your life or your relationships you wish to improve and then link it to the different rooms in your home. When you improve these rooms, you can also improve that area of your relationship.

aspect of your life	aspect of your relationship	most important room or rooms
your physical needs	health, sensuality, sexuality	bedroom, kitchen, bathroom
emotional needs	friendship, intimacy, love	living room, bedroom, bathroom
mental needs	communication, sharing ideas	living room, dining room
spiritual needs	responsibility, privacy	bedroom, all rooms

THE BATHROOM

In most households, the bathroom is a very private space, and we seldom share the time we spend here with others. The bathroom offers us the opportunity to relax and unwind, and gives us time for self-reflection. The water element flows through the bathroom, filling the space with refreshing and cleansing energy. Not only does water purify the body, but it is also cleansing to the mind and spirit. Water energy aids the power of self-expression enhancing your powers of communication.

THE KITCHEN

The kitchen is not only a place for preparing food, but can also be the social center of the home and an area that is filled with love and creativity. In the kitchen, you not only nourish your body, but also show care and attention to yourself, your partner, and family. The earth and wood element flows strongly through the kitchen, and these energies create a feeling of satisfaction and strength.

THE DINING AREA

The dining area is the meeting place of the home, a place that gives you space to catch up on the day's events and to enjoy each other's company. Strong energy in the dining room promotes communication because when you are relaxing during a satisfying meal, your power of expression is enhanced. Like the kitchen, the dining room is filled with earth energy, which has a gathering and binding action, bringing you together.

SEE ALSO

FINDING YOUR STYLE PAGE 18

MINIMALIST OR COZY LIVING? PAGE 20

THE ART OF FENG SHUI PAGE 148

LIGHT AND COLOR PAGE 150

ENTRANCE HALL

LIVING ROOM

KITCHEN

BEDROOM

BATHROOM

DISCUSSION

FOCUS

INSPIRATION

INTERACTION

finding your style

FINDING YOUR STYLE CAN TAKE YOU ON A RELATIONSHIP-STRENGTHENING JOURNEY, DEEPENING YOUR IDENTITY AS A COUPLE OR AS HOMESHARERS. HAVING A CENTRAL THEME MAKES THE PROCESS OF PLANNING AND DECORATING YOUR SPACE A MUCH MORE CREATIVE AND ENJOYABLE EXPERIENCE TO SHARE. SEEING YOUR IDEAS TAKE FORM IS AN EMPOWERING ACT, WHICH IS AN EXCELLENT WAY OF IMPROVING THE WAY THAT YOU AND YOUR HOMESHARERS INTERACT WITH EACH OTHER.

The style of your home and its decoration has an impact on how you view yourselves and how you use your place. For example, a cozy space filled with soft furnishings will suit a couple who spend time at home and whose life centers around the family, while a home with more open-plan living and the maximum space for entertaining will encourage the occupants to enjoy an outgoing and sociable lifestyle.

Most people naturally choose objects, furnishings, and colors that best express their personality and attitude to life—so the style of the home usually develops naturally over time. We are usually attracted to the style of home that best reflects our personal image and our lifestyle. Your choice of decorating style is therefore closely connected to the location and architectural features of the building itself. If you live in a country house, it is more likely that you will feel comfortable with a traditional country look, but if you are townhouse or loft dwellers you may prefer a more contemporary style. This does not necessarily mean that country people do not like urban interiors or vice versa.

While the structure and age of your home may provide you with the raw ingredients for a design style, everybody has their own way of mixing them together and adding their own special flavor.

Successful decorating schemes are often an eclectic mixture of styles using both old and new furniture and furnishings. There is no rule to say that you cannot mix and match styles, and most successful interiors introduce elements from outside influences.

PERSONAL PREFERENCES

THESE QUESTIONS HELP YOU DECIDE THE CHARACTER AND FEELING OF YOUR HOME INTERIOR.	person A	person B	person C
Would you describe yourselves as…			
sporty			
artistic			
sophisticated			
traditional			
Do you want your home to be…			
a calm sanctuary			
dramatic and inspirational			
bright and friendly			
Do you prefer rooms to be…			
open and spacious			
cozy and comfortable			
Do you prefer			
warm colors			
cool colors			
Do you like			
rich, strong colors			
light, pale colors			
Do you have privacy and a personal space?			

Like relationships, decorating your home involves having an open mind and a certain amount of flexibility. By experimenting and showing a willingness to change things around if you don't get it right the first time, you will increase the reward and satisfaction of creating a beautiful home.

Finding a style that suits both partners or all homesharers can create a strong sense of common aims and interests. It may be that you are all attracted to a particular place you have visited, and this sets the scene for your home style. For example, you may feel attracted to the strong rich colors and earthy interiors of Mexican homes, or you may pre-fer the old-world charm of a traditional colonial building. Couples may share a love for a particular time in history, which can often lead to recreating a style and collecting objects related to the period.

Styles can be interpreted in many different ways, and often the solution lies in the ambience and architecture of the rooms themselves. If you want an oriental look, an opulent Chinese style with rich colors and lacquered furniture would suit a large period home. A simple Japanese style with plenty of wood and plain surfaces would be more appropriate to a contemporary apartment. Use the following questionnaires to help you.

CREATE A COLLAGE

The best way to identify a style that suits you both as a couple or all of you as homesharers is to look for colors, styles, objects, homes, and places that appeal to you. Collect a number of books, magazines, color charts, and fabric samples to use as sources of inspiration and to clarify your preferences. Cut out or photocopy pictures that you like; then put them together to make up a collage on a large piece of paper. Give each person the freedom to contribute his or her own ideas. You might find that the finished collage has a consistent style or that the different elements work well together. If the styles contrast badly, the collage can be a good starting point for a compromise.

LIFESTYLE

THESE QUESTIONS HELP YOU TO DECIDE ON THE FOCUS OF YOUR MAIN ROOMS AND THE ARRANGEMENT AND LAYOUT OF SPACE AND FURNITURE IN YOUR HOME. YOUR LIFESTYLE WILL ALSO LARGELY INSPIRE THE SHAPES, PATTERNS, AND MATERIALS IN YOUR HOME FURNISHINGS.

	person A	person B	person C
Do you lead a…			
relaxed lifestyle			
pressured lifestyle			
Do you do much entertaining at home?			
What activities do you do together most often in your living room?			
Do you enjoy outdoor living?			
Do you spend much time at home alone?			
Do you have any special interests that you share?			
Do you eat in the…			
kitchen			
dining room			
living room			
Are you more interested in…			
town pursuits			
country pursuits			

INSPIRATION

THESE QUESTIONS HELP YOU FIND SPECIFIC THEMES FOR YOUR DECORATING SCHEME AND ALSO GIVE YOU CLUES TO THE DIFFERENT COLORS, SHAPES, AND FURNISHING STYLES YOU CAN INTRODUCE.

	person A	person B	person C
Where do you like to go on vacation?			
Do you have an affinity with any particular place or culture?			
Do you like any specific time in history?			
Do you have any special hobbies or interests?			
Which famous paintings do you like?			
Have you any special ornament, object, or heirloom that you particularly like?			

minimalist or cozy living?

MANY PEOPLE ARE DRAWN TO THE MINIMALIST STYLE. A CLEAN AND CLUTTER-FREE HOME CAN BE THE PERFECT ANTIDOTE TO THE BUSTLE AND NOISE OF THE MODERN WORLD. IN IT YOU CAN FIND PEACE AND TRANQUILITY AND AN ENVIRONMENT THAT IS HEALTHY AND STRESS RESISTANT. BUT DON'T CHOOSE AN ELEGANT MINIMALIST STYLE AT THE EXPENSE OF YOUR HOME COMFORTS.

A minimal interior may be the perfect retreat for people who lead busy and hectic lives as it helps to simplify life and reduce extraneous distractions. However, to live successfully in a minimal home, both partners need to be neat and organized. In a pristine home every bit of dust shows up, and even the odd bit of clutter can spoil the effect.

Minimal homes are likely to appeal to art lovers and intellectuals who are more interested in mental stimulation than physical comforts. Stylish and sophisticated couples also relish a minimal home, which they appreciate for the simplicity of form and the space around them.

Overall, a minimal home is less sensual than a home in which there is emphasis on comfort and color. Couples who prefer a minimal interior are more likely to have a relationship based on intellectual rather than physical compatibility. This does not mean that you can't enjoy sensual love if you live in a minimalist home. There are many ways to create a romantic atmosphere, and a minimal interior can quickly be transformed with the addition of soft lighting or a sheepskin rug.

Minimal style can run from austere rooms to a cozier, friendlier interpretation that uses clean lines and subdued colors.

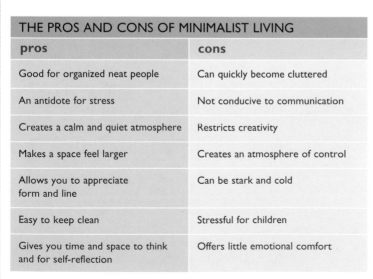

THE PROS AND CONS OF MINIMALIST LIVING	
pros	**cons**
Good for organized neat people	Can quickly become cluttered
An antidote for stress	Not conducive to communication
Creates a calm and quiet atmosphere	Restricts creativity
Makes a space feel larger	Creates an atmosphere of control
Allows you to appreciate form and line	Can be stark and cold
Easy to keep clean	Stressful for children
Gives you time and space to think and for self-reflection	Offers little emotional comfort

You should think twice about creating a minimal home if there are children living with you. Children need visual and tactile stimulation to aid their physical and mental development. A very controlled environment can act as a form of sensory deprivation, having long-lasting emotional and mental effects.

creating comfort

It is possible to live in a well-designed and functional home without it being totally minimal. Modern buildings and contemporary furniture have clean lines and simple shapes that help to create an airy and harmonious living space without being overly cluttered.

TEST YOUR MINIMALIST / COZY CREDENTIALS

GIVE YOURSELF A RATING BETWEEN 1 AND 10 ON THE FOLLOWING TO FIND OUT WHETHER A MINIMAL OR COZY INTERIOR STYLE IS BETTER SUITED TO YOUR PERSONALITY, LIFESTYLE, AND RELATIONSHIP. ADD UP THE TOTAL SCORE FOR THE ODD- AND EVEN-NUMBERED QUESTIONS SEPARATELY.

		person A	person B	person C	person D
1	an organized/neat person				
2	a creative person				
3	a stylish and sophisticated person				
4	an emotional or sentimental person				
5	a person with an analytical and logical mind				
6	a physically active person				
7	an art lover and/or collector				
8	a person who prefers traditional style				
ODD AND EVEN QUESTIONS SCORE:					

PEOPLE WHO SCORE HIGHER ON THE ODD-NUMBERED QUESTIONS THAN ON THE EVEN-NUMBERED QUESTIONS MAY WELL BE SUITED TO USING A MINIMAL STYLE IN THEIR HOME. THE HIGHER THE SCORE FOR THE ODD-NUMBERED QUESTIONS, THE MORE MINIMAL YOU CAN GO. IF YOU SCORED HIGHER ON THE EVEN-NUMBERED QUESTIONS, THE CHANCES ARE THAT YOU WILL NOT BE HAPPY OR COMFORTABLE WITH A MINIMAL STYLE. TRY SOMETHING A BIT MORE ENGAGING.

TIPS FOR CREATING COZY SPACES IN YOUR HOME

A window seat allows you to view the world from a place of safety.

A chaise longue in your bedroom for day lounging.

A four-poster bed can offer you a room within a room.

A beanbag or floor cushions in a spare room can become a cozy retreat.

A garden shed, tree house, or gazebo is hidden away from view.

A soft, fluffy terrycloth robe can offer you an instant circle of security.

SEE ALSO

FINDING YOUR STYLE PAGE 18

CHOOSING COLOR PAGE 22

STARTING WORK PAGE 140

THE ART OF FENG SHUI PAGE 148

choosing color

COLOR CREATES IMPACT AND ATMOSPHERE, AND IS USUALLY THE FIRST THING THAT PEOPLE NOTICE WHEN ENTERING A ROOM. IN ADDITION TO BEING GOOD TO LOOK AT, COLOR HAS MOOD-ENHANCING QUALITIES, SO IT IS IMPORTANT THAT WE SURROUND OURSELVES WITH COLORS THAT NURTURE US AND THAT WE LIKE.

Strong, rich colors create an atmosphere that we can pick up immediately, while the effects of softer tones take longer for us to notice. Also, the colors in the rooms where we spend a long time will have a more profound and lasting effect on our moods than those in areas we just pass through.

In order to relax and feel comfortable, you need to find a color scheme that all the occupants like. If a room is decorated in colors that make someone feel uncomfortable, they will instinctively try to avoid spending time there. If you are constantly surrounded by colors you do not like, you are likely to become irritable and quick to lose your temper. Social studies have found that arguments are much more likely to start up in the areas of the house decorated in colors that one partner dislikes.

color families

Colors can be linked to different personality traits, and so our favorite hues can tell us a great deal about ourselves. We all have a color identity and belong to a color family. By finding these colors, you will be able to come to a better understanding of yourself, your home, and your relationships.

To find out which color family you belong to, decide which color you think best reflects your personality. This color will indicate the color family you belong to.

YELLOW FAMILY

The yellow family is happy, sociable, and outgoing. They are friendly people who are clever and bright. People of this family like intellectual stimulation and to exchange ideas. Their home should be light and bright, and give them the opportunity to socialize and communicate. The yellow family can be highly creative, but with a practical streak. If you belong to this family, you will be full of ideas for home decorating and good at planning and organizing your home.

GREEN FAMILY

The color green is a mixture of blue and yellow, so this color family reveals a combination of character traits. On one hand, the green personality is calm and quiet; on the other they enjoy social interaction. They prefer spending time with one other person rather than a big group, so they put time and energy into their relationships. The home is very important to the green family, and they like to be settled, secure, and surrounded by personal items.

RED FAMILY

If you belong to the red family group, you are likely to have an outgoing and active personality. Red people understand action more than words and often take the lead in a relationship. They have strong personalities and will power, so they are good at seeing things through to the end. Red family members need a stimulating and dramatic environment. The best way to relate to people from this family is by doing things together—a decorating project would be ideal.

RED-ORANGE

BLUE-GREEN

BLUE

BLUE FAMILY

Blue family members are calmer and quieter than the other three groups. Often these people are introverted and prefer a peaceful life. They also prefer to spend more time on their own and use their home as a retreat and private sanctuary. The blue family member needs privacy in their home and intimate spaces where they can relax.

creating color harmony

It is a good idea to have the color family of all homesharers represented in your home. If you share the same color family, introduce these colors into your living spaces. If your colors are not harmonious, find a neutral color that is pleasing and compatible with the color identities of all occupants.

When choosing a color scheme, you will need to consider the amount of light, warmth, and size of a room, as well as your personal preferences. Warm colors like red, orange, gold, and yellow will make even the coldest room look warm and cozy, and have a stimulating effect. Warm colors are most suitable for activity areas or in rooms that are cold or lack natural light. At the other end of the scale, blue and green are cooling colors. They are useful for decoration of small or sunny rooms and to create spaciousness.

The third group of tones are the neutrals. These include beige, tan, cream, and off-white. Neutrals are important tones as they can provide a good backdrop for several strong and contrasting colors or can be used alone to create a subtle, relaxing atmosphere. Black, white, and gray can be dramatic, but too severe to live with without using touches of bright or light accent colors.

color and your relationship

Color is a universal language that reveals messages from your psyche. Your favorite colors can reveal your strengths and weaknesses, and help you understand your relationships with partners, family, and friends. You will naturally feel a deep connection with people from the same color family as yourself, so you will also have a natural empathy and understanding of what makes each other tick. If your partner belongs to the color family lying alongside yours on the color wheel, you will also have a natural closeness and common outlook on life. Colors that lie opposite each other on the wheel show relationships that can be complementary, but can also be at odds with one another. Partners from these opposite families need to work hard at respecting each other's differences and finding their own space within the relationship.

SEE ALSO

THE HEALTHY HOME PAGE 14

FINDING YOUR STYLE PAGE 18

LIGHT AND COLOR PAGE 150

SOUND THERAPY PAGE 154

your changing needs

A CHANGE IN CIRCUMSTANCES OFTEN TRIGGERS A DESIRE TO REORGANIZE OR CHANGE OUR HOME IN SOME WAY. THIS NATURAL DESIRE TO REDECORATE OR EVEN MOVE HOUSE ALTOGETHER REFLECTS OUR INSTINCTIVE NEED FOR OUR HOME TO SUPPORT OUR LIFESTYLE—ESSENTIAL IF OUR HOME IS TO PROVIDE THE SPACE AND SUPPORTIVE ATMOSPHERE APPROPRIATE TO OUR SITUATION.

During our lives, we go through many stages, and our ideas about who we are and what we should be doing change from time to time. As we travel our path in life, we find ourselves in different situations and relationships. At certain stages we may live alone; at others we may share our home with another person or a group of people. There are new arrivals, too, and often couples have to accommodate new family members. There is the arrival of a new baby, an elderly relative may need care and move in with you, or your financial circumstances may require you take in lodgers or rent out part of your home for support.

Your home needs attention if it is to accommodate a changing family structure. Often, this means you should turn your attention to changing the use of various rooms and reorganizing the management of your home. A healthy home is never static or completed. A home should grow with time. By assessing and taking action before your new living arrangements become stressful, you will create an environment that will help you to adapt to the new living arrangements.

A bit of forethought and preparation will help make a new arrival in the family a happy rather than a stressful event. If the new arrival is a baby, you need to get as much done as possible before he or she arrives.

Pets bring life and energy into a home. This energy needs to be channeled into appropriate areas within the home and times. Setting out some simple rules early will help the pet to fit in with other homesharers.

ADAPTING TO PETS

Make a quick checklist for establishing different areas in your home such as Messy and Clean, Activity and Quiet. These give you a clear set of rules that you can communicate to your pet. Dogs can usually be trained to keep out of particular rooms or areas. Cats, on the other hand, are a bigger challenge.

moving home

The first thing we do when we move house is to imprint our identity onto a new home. We rarely feel truly relaxed in spaces decorated and filled with other people's furniture and furnishings, especially if we are intending to stay there for some time. Even when living in a rented place, most people like to add the finishing touches, such as hanging their own pictures and placing their own ornaments around the space.

Moving to a new home with a partner is an exciting moment. No matter how well you know each other, an unfamiliar space brings with it new challenges and also the opportunity to renew and develop your relationships.

Bringing elements of your past with you to a new home can help you retain a sense of who you are, but you should also be willing to look to the future and create an environment that enables you both to move on and grow together.

adapting to children

If you are a couple with children or are likely to have children in the future, it is a good idea to decide which rooms and spaces in your home are likely to be used by children.

Although it would be lovely to think that children would stay in their own play areas, it is a fact of life that they usually prefer to be where adults are. So, if you have children, it is a good idea to combine practicality with style in communal areas. Remember that, like adults, children need their own private spaces, too. They also need boundaries laid out for them. Knowing exactly which areas are safe to play in and which rooms are for quiet makes the home a familiar and secure place to be. If rules are established early on, children will not see them as strict, but will accept them as the natural way of the home.

pets

The arrival of a new pet is always an exciting event for a household. If you wish to continue the relationship in a happy way, you need to establish rules at the onset. Like children, pets need to have physical limits set out for them—places they can go and places that are forbidden. These routines and rules are not meant as a punishment, but help the animal to fit in with the family.

By establishing which areas of your home are messy and which are clean, you can quickly decide where you should allow your pet free access, where they should be fed and sleep, and where they should not go. This will keep your home clean and your pets will not become a subject of contention.

...and if you need your peace and quiet don't forget to plan in a personal space to escape from the turmoil—if only for a few moments.

DESIGNING WITH CHILDREN IN MIND

1 You need good storage in rooms frequented by children so you can quickly clear toys away.

2 Clutter should also be kept to a minimum so you minimize breakage and dirty finger marks.

3 It is wise to have large comfortable sofas and chairs with removable washable covers.

4 Have upholstered furniture treated with stain-resistant finishes.

5 Throws are useful removable accessories that will protect your seating areas from spilled food and drink.

6 Choose painted surfaces that can easily be cleaned.

7 Small children spend a great deal of time on the floor, so make sure the floor is safe from hazards such as exposed sockets and wood that splinters.

8 Make sure steps, stairs, and fireplaces are well guarded.

moving in together

MORE AND MORE COUPLES ARE MOVING IN TOGETHER AFTER BEING USED TO THEIR OWN SPACE. MERGING TWO HOUSEHOLDS INTO ONE CAN BE A DAUNTING AND DIFFICULT TASK. YOU NEED TO INTEGRATE YOUR LIVES AND PERSONAL ITEMS HARMONIOUSLY IF YOU ARE TO ENJOY A HAPPY HOME TOGETHER.

There always comes a time when we have to commit to the future and let go of the past. If you really want to make a relationship work, you need to get rid of possessions that do not foster self-development or enhance your relationship. Your relationship will suffer if one person has all their clutter in the home. Here are some ways to come to amicable decisions on clutter.

equal shares

If space is at a premium, you will both have to compromise and agree to bring a limited number of items with you. Depending on the size of your new home, get a number of large boxes and divide them up equally between you. If you have more items than your quota, you need to make other arrangements for storing the excess away from the house. You could allocate a specific room or storage area in a garage, attic, or cellar for each person's use. Once you have filled your area, you need to find alternative space for the remainder.

Moving in together is always a crucial time for a relationship. The keys to making it a success are open discussion and compromise. A good start at this point will give your home life together solid and healthy foundations.

action: streamline your possessions

The best way of merging two households is for each of you to make a list of individual pieces of furniture and other items in each room. Alongside each item you would like to keep you need to put a check. Next to the items you wish to get rid of, put a cross. Compare your lists and find ways to sort out your differences. Try to come to an equal sacrifice on each side.

Once you have come to an agreement on what should stay and what should go, agree the best way of disposal. Some items could be given to friends and family members; others could be given to thrift stores or sent to an auction. The remaining items need to be thrown away properly.

A NEED FOR PRIVACY

Everyone needs personal space, even couples, and it is essential that each person has a place in the home that they can make their own. If the home is large enough, all the occupants should have a special room, such as a study, sewing room, or den, where they can enjoy a special interest without being disturbed or having to clean up to accommodate others. Even in a small home, you can achieve the same effect. A desk by a window or a special chair in a corner can easily become a personal space. Good time management can also play an important role, giving you time and space to enjoy your home when no one else is around.

In a busy household, the bathroom is often the only place you can lock yourself away for a quiet read or contemplation. However, when shared space is taken over by one person, relationships in the home can become tense and strained. If your home has only one bathroom, it may be a good idea to agree on times when you can use it to relax and not be disturbed (see bathroom schedule maker, page 135).

letting go

Hand over decisions on your own excess objects to your partner. If there are any items that are larger or take up more room than your personal quota, you should agree that your partner has the final say whether something goes or stays.

negotiation

In any decision-making process, the ability to negotiate can be the key. For example, if you have a large surfboard or skis that do not fit into your allocated storage area, you must seek a place to keep them that won't infringe on the living spaces. If you have located a suitable storage area, negotiate with your partner as to the feasibility of using this space. During the negotiation you may need to do a trade and leave some other items behind in exchange for keeping this particular item. Remember that you may not get exactly what you want, but it is also very likely that, very soon, different things will become important to you and you will be pleased to have made the compromise.

placing possessions

Once you have agreed on which personal items you are keeping, you need to find an appropriate place to put them in your new home. Items that you both like, bought, or collected together are best located in shared spaces, as are personal collections that you both like. If you have a collection that your partner does not like, you need to find a personal space in your home where you can store and view it. Small items can usually be hidden away in a cupboard or drawer, or stored in a trunk or box, but larger items need a home in a shed, attic, or garage.

moving into your partner's home

It is often difficult to move into another person's space, even if it belongs to a loving partner. The person who lives there will inevitably have created his own little world. His home will be filled with the things he likes and the colors that please him, and he will have organized himself in the way that suits his lifestyle. Above all, he is likely to have established his own rituals, such as leaving the key in a certain place or doing the laundry at a particular time.

The newcomer is at a disadvantage, for there may not be space for all her belongings. The long-term occupant may feel put out as his routine will be disturbed. Both partners need to make compromises and to make room for each other.

TWO HOUSEHOLDS INTO ONE

If you are combining two existing households, it is best to decide what style and atmosphere you wish to create before you decide which items to keep or get rid of (see Finding your Style, page 18). This will help you work together to form a new look and will also help you to see yourselves as a couple.

Any close relationship is made up of give and take. Each partner needs to feel equally relaxed and in control of the home environment.

action: create space

Discuss exactly what the incoming partner wishes to bring and where these things are going to fit in. Better still, you should consider redecorating and organizing the whole space, so you can start your life together in a revitalized home. Use this book to help you evolve a style of your own.

SEE ALSO

OUR HOMES, OURSELVES PAGE 10

WHERE YOU LIVE PAGE 12

FINDING YOUR STYLE PAGE 18

SHARING A HOME PAGE 28

sharing a home

HOMES ARE NOT ALWAYS SHARED BY PEOPLE CONNECTED BY CLOSE RELATIONSHIPS. IN THESE SITUATIONS, IT IS CRUCIAL THAT EACH INDIVIDUAL'S NEEDS ARE TAKEN INTO ACCOUNT SO THAT EACH PERSON ENJOYS A NURTURING HOME EXPERIENCE—RATHER THAN A LONG-RUNNING ORDEAL TO FIND PRIVACY AND QUIET IN THE HOME.

communal living

People don't always live just with their partner. More and more people these days share their home with friends, homesharers, elderly relatives, or lodgers. In all of these shared situations, it is important to establish which are the common and which are the private areas of the home right from the beginning.

The living room, dining room, and kitchen area are usually communal spaces, and it is important that all the home occupants feel welcome here. Relationships can become strained if some members of your household feel uncomfortable in the shared areas and withdraw to other parts of the house.

One way to bring your homesharers together is to involve everyone in the decorating scheme and to arrange regular get-togethers in your shared spaces.

The bedroom is a private space. Keeping your clothing, photographs, bedtime reading material, and other personal items here can help you to create a sense of security and privacy in even the busiest household.

If you have the space, it is a good idea to create additional areas in the home that are reserved for a particular use, for example, watching TV, studying, or playing. These dedicated areas can be a blessing in homes that include elderly relatives or homesharers with very different interests. Good time management can also help you to enjoy your home when nobody else is around.

To guarantee harmonious living with your fellow homesharers, make sure you agree which are the communal and which are the private areas of your home. Discuss how each communal room should be used and whether or not guests are welcome here.

When the people you share with are just acquaintances, you can work together to make your relationships with each other harmonious.

Your homesharers might not all be human, but they can still be included in the plan for your home.

ATTRACTING NEW ENERGY INTO YOUR BEDROOM	
1	turn your mattress
2	sleep on the other side of the bed
3	buy new sheets and pillowcases
4	burn cleansing aromatic candles in your bedroom
5	get rid of any cuddly toys or seductive underwear that your ex-lover bought you
6	start a new relationship

action: moving on

Discuss which areas of your home you have to share, which areas you wish to share, and which areas you wish to keep private.

Decide on what changes you need to make to your bedroom and whether one or both of you need to move to another room for more privacy.

Arrange a time to spring clean your living room and try out a new layout.

Make a list of those items that hold sentimental value or remind you of your time together.

Decide whether to move, remove, or store.

Discuss and agree on the colors, new furniture, and furnishings in shared spaces.

living together when your relationship is over

Living together as a couple can be a wonderful experience, but it is not always possible to go your separate ways when the relationship is over. It may be that you continue to share your home for financial reasons or through consideration for your children. Whatever the reason for remaining under the same roof, it is essential that your home undergoes some changes to reflect and accommodate the shift in your relationship.

When you were emotionally involved, your home decoration and layout reflected and enhanced your life together. You will have developed sentimental and emotional attachments to your home and to certain objects around you. When you break up, it is important to break these attachments, or you will remain emotionally dependent on each other and find it hard to form new relationships. To help you move on without anger and regret, you should change those aspects of your place that relate to you as a couple.

Clearing out sentimental items and clutter will help you to clear out negative energy that may have been absorbed during times of conflict and unhappiness. The most important areas to cleanse are your living room and bedroom. By spring cleaning your living area, you will be setting the scene for a fresh new life, which will help you live together amicably as friends. Moving your furniture around will also help you dispel old behavior patterns, and by introducing some new items, you can attract some bright new energy into both of your lives.

You also need to consider your sleeping arrangements since one partner will have to move into another bedroom. It is a good idea to have your bedrooms as far apart as possible so you can avoid any embarrassment in the future. Your bed will contain imprints of your previous lover, and you need to pay special attention to clearing these or your future love life may go the same way.

CHAPTER

1

entrances and hallways

THE ENTRANCE IS THE FIRST THING THAT GREETS YOU WHEN YOU COME HOME. LIKE A BOOK COVER, IT SETS

THE TONE FOR YOUR WHOLE EXPERIENCE INSIDE — YOUR ENTRANCE SENDS OUT MESSAGES ABOUT YOU AND

YOUR HOUSEHOLD. THE STYLE, DECORATION, AND COLOR OF YOUR FRONT DOOR CREATES A PICTURE

PROFILE OF YOUR HOME IN JUST A FEW MOMENTS. AN ATTRACTIVE AND WELL-CARED-FOR ENTRANCE TO A

HOME CAN BE MOOD ENHANCING, BUT SETTING THE TONE FOR YOUR HOMECOMING GOES BEYOND THE

FRONT DOOR. A GARAGE, PATH, AND ENTRANCE PORCH ARE ALL FEATURES THAT WELCOME YOU HOME,

AND THE HALL HELPS YOU FORGET THE OUTSIDE WORLD AND FOCUS ON BEING AT HOME.

entrances and hallways

YOUR RELATIONSHIP WITH YOUR HOME IS A VERY STRONG AND INTIMATE ONE. YOUR ENTRANCE SHOULD BE AN "ENTRANCING" PLACE THAT ALLURES AND DRAWS YOU IN. IT IS A PLACE OF PROMISES, GIVING YOU A TASTE OF WHAT LIES WAITING FOR YOU INSIDE—COMFORT, A RETREAT FROM THE OUTSIDE WORLD, AND A PLACE TO RELAX.

The way you feel about your home when you first chose it can be compared to the feelings you experienced when you first met your partner. You may have felt a strong feeling of attraction, or perhaps you just felt relaxed and comfortable with each other. An attractive entrance should stimulate similar feelings of anticipation and comfort, making your homecoming a pleasure and bringing a smile to your face.

Perhaps you were first drawn to the style and architecture of your home, or it may have been the beautiful surroundings or picturesque view. If you live in a townhouse or apartment, its convenient location or its exciting and modern features may have given it the "wow" factor. Realtors will tell you that they know within the first minute whether a potential buyer will actually like a property. This indicates how important first impressions are and in particular the effect of the approach and the front door itself. The outside entrance to your home should have just the right feel and should resonate with you if you are to feel happy when you walk into it.

The outside of your home should be a pleasure to look at and have a personality of its own. The architecture, shapes, color, and proportions of the windows and doors all contribute to creating a pleasing effect. Unfortunately, many houses have been spoiled by the replacement of windows and doors with ones that are out of keeping with the original building style and materials. So while it is a good idea to personalize your entrance in your own favorite colors and style, they should be in synch with the age and building style of your home.

It is not just the physical appearance of a building that makes a home attractive. The atmosphere in a place is often created by the previous occupants so the building itself seems to exude its own energy. Even new buildings take on a life force of their own, and often these places hold an air of mystery and fascination for us—as if they are waiting for us to make our mark.

clutter in entrance

Entrances announce that you are home and should give you a big welcome. When you pass through these places, you should breathe a sigh of relief and be thankful that you are home. So it is important that the entrance to your home is attractive and well cared for. The way you maintain your entrance sends out messages about the way you care for your home and yourself.

If the entrance is messy and unsightly or strewn with obstacles, this will send out negative messages about your home. If your gate is broken and your front yard is overgrown,

The entrance to your home should reflect your personal style, letting you know that you are entering a safe and familiar space. This example uses glass walls to make a subtle transition between the interior and the exterior of the home.

not only will it cause an obstruction getting to your front door, it may also mirror a household where there are difficulties and perhaps obstructive relationships. A dark, depressing entrance will put you in a dark and depressed mood, and you will find it much harder to relax and enjoy being home. If you are not pleased to be home, your attitude and behavior will not be conducive to meeting and

greeting your partner. Clutter around your front door is also likely to put you in a bad mood. Stepping over obstacles, such as flowerpots, children's toys, or bicycles, can point to messy and disorganized relationships in the home. Not only are you likely to feel irritated by the objects in question, but your feelings will extend to the person they belong to. This is particularly trying on relationships where several people share a common entrance.

your hallway

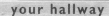

It is in the entrance hall that you are truly welcomed home. Here, you may be greeted by your partner, child, or even your pet. So the hall is a place that makes you feel a valued and important member of the household. It is in the entrance porch or hall that you adjust yourself from being in a public to being in a private place, so it is most important that your entrance sends out the right signals—offering you a sanctuary from the outside world and promising comfort and relaxation.

The transition between the home and the outside should not be abrupt, and even when you have stepped inside your front door, you need an in-between space where you can orientate yourself and change your focus from outside to inside. The entrance hall creates the opportunity for you to come down to earth so you can focus your attention on being at home. Making this area a cheerful and organized place is a way of greeting yourself and your partner or other people that you live with each day.

Outdoors, we have to protect ourselves against the elements and harsh environmental conditions, but inside we can connect to our true selves and shed our outer defenses. In many cultures, people remove their shoes in

the hall before entering the home. This is both a practical and a symbolic ritual. Taking off your coat and shoes means that the dirt clinging to these items remains in the porch or outer area. At the same time, you symbolically leave behind all associations with the outside world.

Walking barefoot on your floor or changing into soft slippers can also help you literally "touch base" and adapt to the atmosphere in your home. Connecting yourself to the floor provides a very soothing and earthing feeling, especially after work. The grounding helps relax the mind, which is often overstimulated during the day. It will put you in touch with the important things in life, one's partner, family, and home, and this can help you channel new energy into your relationships. It is not essential for you to take off your shoes in your hall in order to benefit from its grounding qualities. A hall decorated in warm earthy colors and with a natural wood or ceramic tile floor would have a similar "earthing" effect.

TIME TO REMEMBER

Think of the first impressions of your present home and what attracted you to it. Was it the location, appearance, or atmosphere that had the strongest effect on you? If you are moving to a new home, make a list of what qualities you are looking for and how they may differ from your present home.

SEE ALSO ─◯

WHERE YOU LIVE PAGE 12 ─◯

THE HEALTHY HOME PAGE 14 ─◯

FRONT DOORS PAGE 34 ─◯

LIGHT AND COLOR PAGE 150 ─◯

AN EASTERN VIEW

Feng shui experts believe that if your front door is narrow, it will constrict the chi entering the home and the occupants of the home will be prone to petty arguments. If you have to bend your head to enter your front door, this will restrict and limit your vision, making it more difficult to see your partner's point of view. A broken or poorly fitting front door will create an insecure and shaky relationship.

The perfect welcome. The entrance to your home sets the tone for your whole experience while you are there. It should offer you a glimpse of the comforts, calm, and happiness that wait for you inside.

front doors

THE FRONT DOOR IS ALWAYS OF GREAT SIGNIFICANCE IN A HOME: IT IS THE THRESHOLD THAT DIVIDES THE OUTSIDE WORLD AND THE INNER, PRIVATE WORLD. IT PROVIDES YOU WITH A MEANS OF CONNECTION WITH THE OUTSIDE WORLD, BUT ALSO OFFERS YOU A WAY TO SHUT IT OUT. THIS MEANS THAT YOUR FRONT DOOR CAN BE SEEN AS YOUR GREATEST ALLY, PROTECTING YOUR HOME FROM UNWELCOME VISITORS AS WELL AS ACTING AS AN ESSENTIAL PART OF YOUR WELCOMING RITUAL TO ALL YOU INVITE INTO YOUR HOME.

The front door is the protector of the home, keeping out wind and weather as well as strangers and uninvited guests. When you step through the front door into your home, you know that you have arrived in a welcoming and safe place. When shut, the front door provides a sense of security and separation from the outside world.

Through your front door, you invite positive energy (chi) into your home. This flows in from the natural surroundings and also comes from thoughts and feelings created by the people you invite to enter your personal space. In Far Eastern cultures, it is traditional for the front door to face the rising sun and be decorated with good luck charms or symbolic colors to ward off evil. If you are replacing a front door or creating a new one, it is worth considering the importance of creating a threshold that affords the right energy for you and your partner or family.

creating the right message

Whatever message your front entrance gives to other people, it is important that your front door gives you a special hello. Create an entrance and front door area that speaks to you and says something about the way you wish to view your home. Customizing your entrance means it will have a special meaning.

color speak

If you remember nothing else about a front door, you will remember its color. This is because color has a very strong visual impact. Colors also have symbolic meanings linked to our individual personal, religious, social, or cultural associations.

When you return home, ask yourself whether you get a welcoming feeling or whether you get no feeling at all. You only need to change the color if you feel a strong negative reaction to it. Look at the color of your front door and let the color speak to you. What word or feelings comes to mind? Perhaps your front door is bright yellow, a color that sends out the message of a happy, sunny home. A dark blue or black door could say that the occupants are quiet or reclusive and do not wish to be disturbed by the outside world.

If you decide that your front door needs a change of color, you need to agree on a color that sends out the right message about your household. If you can't decide, try getting two sets of gloss paint sample charts and cut them up so you have a square of each color listed. Give one set to your partner and turn your backs so you can't see what the other is doing. Arrange the squares in your order of preference. Then, compare your results—your first choice may be different, but you will probably find you both put at least one color fairly high on the list—which gives you a good compromise. Discuss what each color means to you and what it says about your relationship with each other.

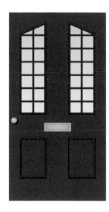

BLACK – serious, wise, adult, and sophisticated. Can also be perceived as threatening, it can keep people away.

WHITE – protective, clear, fair, and strong. Can also be seen as cold and distant, with little sense of fun.

RED – creative, passionate, and dynamic. Red may also signify restlessness and a dislike for peace and quiet.

YELLOW – happy, welcoming, and positive. Finding the right tone is tricky; some yellows are pale and cold.

ORANGE – young, warm, and sociable. Vibrant orange can be offensive to some more conservative people.

DOOR DETECTIVES

It is sometimes difficult to access what your front door says about you, because you know yourselves so well. It is a useful exercise to go for a walk along your street or a street in a different neighborhood and look at other people's front doors and entrances. Ask yourselves what word or emotion comes to mind when looking at different doors. One door might say "nice to see you" while another may say "go away."

GREEN – honest, healthy, and friendly. Green is also a calm color that can be read as boring and unexciting.

TURQUOISE – mixing blue and green, turquoise is a calming, meditative color that exudes a peaceful air.

BLUE – relaxing, calm, and quiet. Can be unwelcoming to visitors, but serves to calm you as you enter the home.

PURPLE – between red and blue, purple mixes restful, spiritual qualities with creative and friendly impulses.

PINK – lively, fun, and caring. Pink shares qualities with red, but can be seen as a childish or immature color.

storage and sharing a space

HALLS, PASSAGES, AND STAIRWAYS ARE THE ARTERIES OF YOUR HOME, GIVING YOU ACCESS AND LINKING DIFFERENT AREAS TOGETHER. WHILE YOU ARE MOVING THROUGH THE HALL YOU WILL BECOME AWARE OF THE ATMOSPHERE IN YOUR HOME. IT IS A PLACE WHERE YOUR SENSES BECOME ALERT, TESTING THE AIR FOR A HINT OF WHAT IS GOING ON INSIDE. PERHAPS YOU CAN SMELL A CUP OF COFFEE BREWING OR HEAR FAMILIAR VOICES.

It is important that your hallway is organized to make your homecoming a smooth and positive event. A hall needs a lot of storage facilities, because it usually acts as a dumping ground for objects brought in from outside. If it is your only "wet" area, you will have to provide somewhere to keep boots, coats, and hats as well as somewhere to put umbrellas, walking canes, keys, and mail. Some households also keep strollers and shopping trolleys in the front hall, and these larger items often lead to an overcrowded and messy space. If you walk into a hall and there is nowhere to put your coat or you cannot find your keys, this will not put you in the best of moods. This creates stress on entering and exiting the home.

Obviously halls vary greatly in size, and you have to balance needs with practicality. It is always worth discussing what you need to store in your hall with homesharers, and if there is not enough room, find other accessible storage areas nearby. It is also a good idea to decide where to keep essential items like the mail or car keys and stick to them.

welcoming arms

It can be quite a challenge to find unusual and inspirational ways to store essential items. I have a friend who is a collector of Far Eastern art and sculpture, and in his hall is a beautiful life-size bronze sculpture of a man with hands raised. One day when we

---

ENHANCE THE EARTH ENERGY

PROMOTING THE FLOW OF EARTH ENERGY THROUGH YOUR ENTRANCE AND HALLWAY WILL HELP EVERYONE WHO ENTERS YOUR HOME FEEL WELCOMED. TRY THESE SUBTLE TECHNIQUES FOR CREATING A WARM AND RELAXED ATMOSPHERE:

■ Aromatic shrubs or plants near the front door will slow you down and put you in a calm mood.

■ A stone or tile floor will help you adapt smoothly from the outside world to the atmosphere within the house.

■ A musical doorbell will make the home feel more welcoming to visitors.

■ Soft earthy colors, such as terracotta, will have a warming and grounding effect.

■ An uncluttered hall will help bring good chi into your home.

■ A ceramic or stone sculpture will change your focus as you enter the home.

Warm wood tones and matching carpet create a welcoming, natural atmosphere in this hallway. Innovative storage units make maximum use of the space available under the stairs, avoiding clutter and obstruction.

returned to his apartment, I was surprised when my friend casually tossed his hat over one hand and hung his coat over the other arm. He then happily proceeded to empty the contents of his pocket into a valuable Ming bowl on the side table.

sharing a hall

Sharing your home is never easy, but you can avoid a great deal of conflict if you dedicate separate entrances to different people. This way, each person can create their own type of welcome and feel that they have a special place of their own. Above all, having your own front door and hall gives you privacy and makes your relationship autonomous. In many homes, though, having a separate entrance for each resident is simply not feasible. If you do have to share a hallway with someone with whom you do not have a close personal relationship, such as a lodger or perhaps an ex-partner, there are many things you can do to promote a smooth flow in and out of your home and reduce mutual disturbance.

The first task is to install a separate doorbell and mail box for each homesharer. There is nothing more annoying than opening the door for other people's guests. It is also a good idea to choose a floor covering in the hall and stairs that absorbs sound, so you minimize the disturbance caused by the coming and going of other residents.

Making sure that a shared entrance is clear of clutter, attractive, and welcoming goes a long way to harmonizing relationships where there are a number of people in the home.

IDEAS FOR SHARED ENTRANCES AND HALLWAYS

HALLWAYS ARE OFTEN NEGLECTED OR IGNORED SPACES WITHIN A HOME, ESPECIALLY WHEN SEVERAL PEOPLE SHARE. AND YET THEY CAN HAVE A HUGE IMPACT ON THE OVERALL IMPRESSION GIVEN BY A HOME, AS WELL AS ON THE RELATIONSHIPS BETWEEN THE HOMESHARERS.

minimize conflict caused by shared entrances by:

1 getting your own mailbox

2 installing a separate door bell with a different chime

3 having a separate coat and hat hook or cupboard

4 having a special place in the hall to leave notes for each other

5 putting your hall light on an automatic timer so it turns itself off

6 deadening sound with a thick hall rug and stair carpet

7 buying a basket in which to put things to be taken upstairs

8 installing footlights on the staircase for coming home at night

SEE ALSO

THE HEALTHY HOME PAGE 14

YOUR CHANGING NEEDS PAGE 24

HALLS OF DISTINCTION PAGE 38

LIGHT AND COLOR PAGE 150

halls of distinction

IT IS WORTH MAKING A FUSS OF YOUR HALL. AFTER ALL, IT WILL BE THE FIRST PART OF YOUR HOME THAT YOU SEE WHEN YOU GET HOME AFTER A BUSY DAY. IT ALSO GIVES VISITORS THEIR FIRST IMPRESSION OF THE INTERIOR OF YOUR HOME. YOU CAN USE COLOR TO CONVEY JUST THE MESSAGE THAT YOU AND YOUR HOMESHARERS WISH TO WELCOME PEOPLE IN.

Although you are constantly moving through the hall, it is not just a passageway leading to somewhere else. The hall gives you and your visitors the first glimpse of your home, and it is important to treat it not only

ing nook. However, you should remember that the hall is the first room you see when entering your home, and whatever use you give to this area will influence your homecoming and therefore the way you view your

Variations of white mean that light is reflected throughout the hall. They also give an uncluttered air, important for a space that is used for frequent comings and goings. One drawback is that some whites can appear cold.

as a utilitarian place, but to give it a distinctive look of its own. With care and attention you can turn your hall into a special area that can say "welcome" in its own unique way. Depending on its shape and size, a hall can become a room with a special purpose. For example, the space below a staircase could be turned into a home office or a secluded eat-

home. In feng shui, it is believed that the first room you see will influence your relationships when you are in the home. If, when you enter, the first room is the kitchen or dining area, your family life will revolve around meals and food. On the other hand, if you have a desk in your hall, you are more likely to have a work-oriented household.

Yellow can be a good, positive color for a hall. Its uplifting effect can put a spring in your step as you leave the home and a smile on your face as you return. It is not a restful color, so avoid it if a calming welcome is what you're after.

colors for halls

The entrance hall is the pivotal point of movement in the home as we pass through this space on our way in and out of the home as well as between rooms and floors.

Halls are fun because we do not spend much time in them, and they can be decorated in much more intense and unusual colors than elsewhere in the home. Color psychologists have found that rich bright colors are mood enhancing and encourage physical movement. Rich red, purple, terracotta, magenta, and gold are vibrant tones that increase your vitality as you move through the space. Should you not wish to use these strong colors on the walls, you could use them to highlight woodwork, or in the flooring, lighting, and other accessories.

For many people, a home is a sanctuary away from the noise and stress of the outside world. If you want to create a more calming and soothing entrance, you should use cooler colors. Try aquamarine, lime green, peacock blue, or pale lilac as these shades, although cool in tone, still have sparkle and life. If you use paints made from natural pigments, bright colors take on a chalky effect and are better suited to more traditional settings. No matter what your color preferences, the hall is the perfect room to indulge your creativity and to try out colors and techniques that you would be too afraid to try elsewhere. Halls can be quite inspirational, and you can turn yours into an art gallery to house and display your special collections. The hall is also a perfect location for an odd piece of furniture or a special object d'art. Let your imagination go and spend an evening brainstorming ideas and themes for your hall.

Blue is a calming, introspective color. In the hall, it will stress the fact that you are back in your own private space. It doesn't reflect light very well and could cause smaller halls to look dark and dingy.

Red is an energizing color that will give a jolt of power as you return home. Depending on the tone that you choose, it can be a very overpowering color. You could just have a small area painted to limit its impact.

Like blue, purple will help you to calm down after a busy day. It is a restful and inner-looking color, but also has that hint of red to bring out dynamic energy. It can be gloomy if used in too small or dark a space. As with red, you could try painting just a small area.

SEE ALSO

CHOOSING COLOR PAGE 22

SHARING A HOME PAGE 28

FRONT DOORS PAGE 34

LIGHT AND COLOR PAGE 150

lighting: creating mood and atmosphere

THE KEY ELEMENT IN CREATING A WELCOMING HALLWAY IS LIGHT. IT IS A GOOD IDEA TO HAVE SEVERAL DIFFERENT LIGHT SOURCES IN YOUR ENTRANCE HALL AND PASSAGEWAY, INCLUDING BOTH NATURAL AND ARTIFICIAL LIGHTING OPTIONS. NATURAL LIGHT ALLOWS YOU TO SEE OUT AND BRINGS AIR AND WARMTH INTO YOUR HOME. BRIGHT ARTIFICIAL LIGHTING GIVES YOU SECURITY, WHILE SOFT LIGHTS CREATE MOOD AND ATMOSPHERE. ALL FORMS OF LIGHT ENCOURAGE CHI ENERGY TO CIRCULATE.

In this apartment electric lighting has been used to create a daylight effect. A plant is also used to bring in a flavor of the outside world.

Where possible, you should try to get natural light into the hall, because it helps you see the weather before you go out as well as allowing you a glimpse inside on your way in. It is ideal if your hall has a window, but if there is no window, light could enter through the front door or a fanlight. A glass panel, if it is patterned or stained, could provide your home with that welcoming glow as well as allowing you to see someone outside. Choose an appealing design that incorporates the sun's rays or another symbol to give you a special welcome home. You could also include your favorite animal, an angel, or a prayer in some way into the design of the door or frame.

Lighting is important in all halls, but especially if you want to make the most of a special feature. In halls with no windows you need to pay special attention to the lighting. It is a good idea to vary the type of lighting as it visually breaks up a long hallway. Install recessed or downlighters flush to the ceiling instead of hanging lights with shades, which blow in the wind and can obstruct your way.

Combine good overhead lighting with wall lights or table lamps on a hall table. They give out a much warmer glow and so are more welcoming than stark overhead lighting. Wall and table lights also give you the opportunity to have a soft light for late homecomings and can be connected to a timer for security when you are away.

IDEAS FOR LIGHTING ENTRANCES AND HALLWAYS

THE KEY TO LIGHTING IN THE HALL IS TO ENSURE THAT THERE IS A GOOD BALANCE BETWEEN THE PRACTICAL AND THE DECORATIVE. IN OTHER WORDS, YOU NEED TO BE ABLE SEE WHERE YOU ARE GOING AND WHO IS COMING IN, BUT YOU SHOULD ALSO TRY TO MAKE THE HALL A WARM-LOOKING AND WELCOMING SPACE BY USING ATMOSPHERIC LIGHTING EFFECTS.

make sure your hall lighting scheme:

1 illuminates the hall so that you can enter without tripping

2 illuminates the entrance so that you can see who is coming in

3 uses a window to allow natural light into the hall or

4 uses glass in the front door or a fanlight to allow light in

5 doesn't use pendant lights that will get in the way

6 uses wall or table lights to produce warm light for atmosphere

7 uses mirrors if the hall is to small or dark to increase space

8 doesn't use mirrors directly opposite the door

using mirrors

Mirrors are functional and dramatically increase the light in a hall, especially when you place them at right angles to the window.

They are especially useful since they increase the feeling of space and double the impact of pictures and ornaments. They are widely used in feng shui because they are said to enhance and direct good energy flow.

We usually look in the mirror to adjust our hair or clothing when we leave the house, and we should remember that we can do the same on our way in. Greeting your loved ones looking disheveled and windswept isn't always the best way to enter your home. So spend a moment looking in the mirror, which will alert you to your mood and help you focus on what your partner will see!

Make sure you hang the mirror so that you can see your whole head in it—it is considered unlucky in feng shui to look into a mirror that cuts off part of your head.

If your hall has a window, it can provide you with a wonderful focal point that would give your hall that mark of individuality. Make the most of a single window by designing an eye-catching window dressing. It could be a traditional style using draped voile or a shimmering sari fabric. For a more modern look, a perforated metal or bamboo blind could be the answer.

WELCOME SYMBOLS	
Two swans	Romantic love
Dolphins	Fidelity
Sun	Happiness
Angel	Protection
Moon	Wisdom
Stars	Destiny
Waves	Freedom
Sunset	Welcome

Cats may be able to see in the dark, but humans can't. The hall must be well lit, especially because it is the site of so much coming and going.

SEE ALSO

FINDING YOUR STYLE · PAGE 18

CHOOSING COLOR · PAGE 22

SHARING A HOME · PAGE 28

LIGHT AND COLOR · PAGE 150

stairs and landing

OFTEN A NEGLECTED AREA, STAIRS FORM THE BACKBONE TO YOUR HOME, PROVIDING A FEELING OF STRENGTH AND SUPPORT. STAIRCASES LINK, BUT ALSO SEPARATE, DIFFERENT LEVELS WITHIN YOUR HOME. OFTEN THEY DEFINE SHARED AND PRIVATE SPACES, AND WHILE MOVING ALONG THE STAIRS AND LANDINGS, YOU CAN VIEW YOUR HOME AND YOUR LIFE FROM DIFFERENT ANGLES.

A good feng shui stairway, carrying energy from the door up into the upper floors of the house. The door can also be seen from all parts of the stairway, another feng shui bonus.

A feature staircase is an asset to any home. The elegant lines lead the eye upward and a smooth handrail is soothing to the touch. Walking up an attractive staircase to different floors can be a very relaxing experience that helps you adjust your attention from activity to the relaxing qualities of more private spaces. Make this change an even more enjoyable experience by lining your staircase with pictures, books, or wall displays.

An open tread staircase or one with open balustrades creates a feeling of light and air. This is especially useful if you have a small entrance hall or if your staircase is part of your main living room. Make sure you have a place to store outdoor clothing in your hall, or the first few steps of the stairway can soon become home to a pile of hats and coats. Long, narrow staircases can be gloomy, uninteresting places, and you need to break the

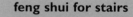

feng shui for stairs

In the ancient art of feng shui, the Chinese believe that the health of the occupants and their relationships is largely dependant on the ability of life-giving chi energy to enter in through the front door and move through the hall and stairs. These are some of the most useful ways of creating good feng shui for stairs:

Narrow twisting staircases should be airy and well lit.

Dark staircases can be improved with the addition of mirrors on the end walls.

A pendulum clock or lava lamp at the bottom of the stairs moves energy up the stairs.

The fire element lifts energy on the stairs, so use fiery colours, such as red and orange, in your decoration.

Open-tread stairs allows energy to escape so place a light under the stairs.

A hanging mobile will circulate energy on a small landing.

Bright, dramatic lighting will energize staircases and a landing.

area up with the help of mirrors, and a variety of lighting, as well as by varying the colors on the stairs and landing.

going up

Accidents can happen on stairs, so make sure you have a good handrail and that the stairs treads are covered in a nonslip material. Although safety is important, lighting does not need to be stark—dramatic lighting can change your mood as you pass through the space. Footlights are both practical and atmospheric and are especially useful if you have to use the staircase at night.

Walking up your staircase can be a whole experience in itself. In many large, traditional family homes, the staircase is wide and sweeping and lined with pictures of the household and family ancestors. The landings often have large windows that flood the stair-well with natural light, creating interesting patterns and shadows throughout the day. At night these staircases are often lit by twinkling chandeliers and candle wall lights. Even if you live in a modest home, you can introduce some of these elements to create a stylish and atmospheric staircase and landing.

A graceful spiral staircase makes a complementary contrast with the straight lines of a minimal apartment. The stairwell allows natural light and energy to flow down into the lower space.

the old and the new

IN THIS ENTRANCE HALL THERE IS A MIXTURE OF OLD AND NEW, WHICH CREATES A BALANCE BETWEEN HOME COMFORT AND INSPIRATION. A FEW WELL CHOSEN ITEMS OF FURNITURE CREATE A STYLISH AND CALM ENTRANCE.

THE FRONT DOOR

Your front door has a very special energy that protects and permeates your home. A good, strong door with good proportions will enhance the quality of your relationship and act as a symbol of your home life. Doors with openings will exert a specific type of energy depending on the shape of the panel. The triangular window in this front door increases the power of the sun as it floods into the home. Triangles and pyramids are renowned for the power they generate as they are able to transform the energy around them. Other shapes have their own specific impact on relationships:

• Circles bring wholeness and harmony.
• Triangles amplify and transform a relationship.
• Diamonds expand and open a relationship to new possibilities.
• Squares provide stability and loyalty.

BALANCE

Entranceways decorated in an eclectic style like the one in the picture reflect a home where the occupants are thoughtful and considerate. Creating a balance in your life and home can be assisted by harmonizing the colors and furnishings in your entrance hall. The glowing wooden door and floor in this modern hall is warm and welcoming, and the deep tones of the wooden storage unit is not only useful, but exudes a quiet strength. Carefully chosen pictures and objects also reflect a caring couple who take their time to get things right both in their home and relationship.

HOW TO CREATE BALANCE

• Use a mixture of warm and cool colors.
• Introduce older-style furniture into a modern setting.
• Keep your entrance free of clutter, but include functional storage and seating.

CLUTTER

When you enter this space, you will feel calm and unhurried as your cares melt away. By keeping this hallway open and uncluttered, you feel that you have time to unwind before you get involved with your home life.

The symmetry of the shapes and cool soothing colors are visually calming. By keeping the central area clutter free, it feels more spacious, so when you move through the hall you get a sense of quiet strength and wisdom.

DECOR

The beauty and colors of natural materials often surpass those we can create from paint and other forms of decoration. The stone floor in this hall gives way to the natural warmth of wood in the inner hall. These are natural materials that ground you when you come home. Natural flooring also helps prepare you for leaving the protection of your place when you go outside. Neutral colors like creamy white and soft cool colors like duck's-egg blue are quiet and thoughtful hues that help relax the mind—especially welcome if you lead a hectic lifestyle. Too much of anything can have a negative impact on your life, and too many cool colors can dampen your enthusiasm for life, and your relationships will suffer. So it is a good idea to introduce a strong warm tone into your hall if you want to boost your interest in your relationships at home.

DECORATING TIPS

• Highlight a special feature in your hallway with a strong bright color.
• The textures and colors of natural materials are natural and comforting.
• An interesting door frame will outline a view into adjoining rooms.
• A simple chair provides a place to sit down and change into your slippers.
• A change in flooring from cool to warm helps the transition from outside to inside.

the gentle welcome

THIS SPACE IS A GREAT EXAMPLE OF THE RULE THAT HALLS NEED TO MAKE AN IMMEDIATE IMPACT. THE INTENSE BLUE OF THE WALLS AND THE PALE WOOD OF THE FLOOR, STAIRS, AND BEAMS MAKE SURE YOU FEEL WELCOME IN THIS HOME.

IMPACT

This modern entrance really has impact. There is no clutter or furnishings in the space, but it certainly is not a minimal one. When you open the door into this modern interior, you will immediately feel the vibrancy and energy of the occupants.

The clean lines, strong colors, and architectural interest reflect a creative couple who have dynamic personalities and individual tastes. The wooden staircase extends the feel-good factor, which attracts you up to more private, intimate spaces. The gently curving path of the corridor offers guests a gentle invitation into the home and keeps it interesting and dynamic. A straight corridor here could have looked threatening, especially with the high ceilings. Light floods in farther down the hall, so we are drawn inward, toward the heart of the home. In all, an enlivening and warm welcome.

CLUTTER

An entranceway free from clutter allows you to focus on the important things in your life without distraction. This entranceway is easy to clean and allows you to move through the space without bumping into furniture. The smooth, rich-toned flooring also allows easy access and avoids stumbling over rugs or mats. When you are able to move freely around your home, your mind becomes relaxed and you are free to focus your attention on your life and relationships. It is a tricky task to get the balance right between a minimal and cluttered entrance. If you remove all furniture and decorative objects, the space can become dead and lifeless. To prevent this, use rich colors and interesting shapes to make up for lack of ornamentation.

FOR CLUTTER FREE

- Moving easily frees up your mind.
- Clutter free minimizes cleaning.
- Creates a soothing atmosphere.

AGAINST CLUTTER FREE

- Having no storage can be irritating.
- Minimal entrances can be uninviting.
- Empty spaces do not enhance good communication.

COLOR

There is a school of thought in interior design that every room should be decorated in the same colors to create a feeling of coherence and space. While this is a good basic rule, it can create a dull environment that does nothing to express your personality. In this home, the intense blue is dramatic but relaxing and gives a sense of space and light. A different color visible in another room creates a sense of mystery and interest, drawing you in.

• Choose strong colors that either contrast or harmonize.

• Choose tones of the same color in different rooms.

• Pale colors in the hall look good when combined with deeper tones in other rooms.

• Dark colors in the hall look good when combined with warm or light colors in other rooms.

• Use the floor coloring to link different rooms when the walls are different colors.

LIGHTING

The colors on your walls reflect light in different ways, and if the space is lit with natural light, the entrance will take on different moods throughout the day. In this hall, the strong architectural shapes of the beam and windows throw interesting patterns and shadows on the floor, so there is no need for furniture and other ornamentation. In the evening this hall is not too brightly lit, so it allows the glow from the other rooms to show through. This gentle welcome will enhance your mood and make you happy to be home.

MAKE THE MOST OF HALL LIGHTING:

• Natural light in the hall helps you adjust to and from the outside world.

• Soft lighting in the hall is more welcoming since it calms you down.

• Changing lighting conditions and shadows makes the hallway a much more interesting space.

assess, discuss, and agree

YOUR ENTRANCE SETS THE TONE FOR YOUR WHOLE EXPERIENCE AT HOME, SO IT IS IMPORTANT TO CREATE A WELCOMING AND ATTRACTIVE SPACE. THIS PAGE WILL HELP YOU ACCESS HOW YOU FEEL ABOUT YOUR ENTRANCES AND HOW YOU USE THEM. IT WILL ALSO HELP YOU FIND WAYS TO IMPROVE THEM.

step one

The first step is to think about the look and feel of your entrance, hall, and stairs. Try the exercises on the Discussion page to get you thinking about the impression your current entrance gives. Then answer the following questions separately and honestly.

BE REALISTIC

Although the process of decorating a space will work better if everyone pulls their weight, you may not find this very easy to achieve. As the instigator, you may find that the bulk of the work for clearing and redecorating the area falls on your shoulders, particularly if you are sharing an entrance with people with whom you do not have a close personal relationship. While this is not ideal, ultimately, it is more important to create a harmonious entrance—and harmonious relationships—rather than trying to force others to do their share. Take consolation in the fact that people will be naturally more inclined to keep the space neat once it is clean and welcoming.

Make sure the entrance to your home is safe for all members of your household. The great outdoors can be tempting for adventurous tykes.

	person A	person B	person C
I think the front door can be improved by:			
being replaced			
being repaired			
being painted			
The entrance to my home is dirty and cluttered and needs clearing up.			
People coming and going disturbs me, so the entrance needs better organization.			
The entrance to my home is unwelcoming and dreary and needs redecorating.			
Our entrance hall is dark and needs more natural light/better lighting.			
I think the entrance hall should have better storage.			
We need more storage for:			
coats/hats/scarves			
bags			
umbrellas			
shoes			
sports equipment			
toys			
bicycles			
keys			
mail			
strollers			
wheelchairs			
other special items			

step two

Many people share their entrances with other people—neighbors, housemates, or other family members. We all like to be welcomed home, so it is important to consult everyone about the use and decoration of a shared entrance. This way, you signal that everyone needs to care for this space and work together to minimize noise and clutter. Mutual respect for shared spaces reflects mutual respect for each other.

discuss and agree

Swap your answers with your partner, which will help you see the situation from his or her point of view.

Some of your answers will probably be the same as your partner, so a good starting point is to discuss the points on which you both agree. Then move on to points of disagreement and try to resolve these so you find a solution that is acceptable to you both.

ANSWER THE FOLLOWING QUESTIONS INDIVIDUALLY, THEN DISCUSS YOUR ANSWERS.	person A	person B	person C
I would like to improve the entrance by:			
clearing and cleaning the entrance			
creating separate storage areas			
installing a new door bell system/video system			
installing new carpeting			
installing new lighting			

ACTION

1	Clear the clutter and clean up your entrance.
2	Carry out your solutions related to shared entrances.
3	Fix anything broken or needing replacement.
4	Move any furniture or furnishings to be replaced.
5	Purchase paints and decorating materials.
6	Arrange a program for building, decoration, or electrical work.
7	Install lights and built-in furniture.
8	Install movable furniture and furnishings.
9	Add finishing touches to your entrance using plants, pictures, and art objects.

discuss and agree

First discuss the points on which you all agree and make a list of the things that need changing and improving. Then discuss your differences by listening carefully to other people's points of view. It is essential that everyone is aware that the entrance is a shared space and should be kept clear of clutter and remain a quiet welcoming place.

step three

Once you have agreed what steps you should take to improve your entrances, you are ready to put your ideas into action. Work out a timetable and plan of action and then delegate the tasks to different people.

CHAPTER

2

living rooms

A STRONG SOURCE OF FIRE ENERGY, THE LIVING ROOM IS THE MOST DYNAMIC AND ACTIVE AREA OF THE

HOME AND FULFILLS MANY FUNCTIONS. SOMETIMES IT IS THE SOCIAL CENTER, AT OTHER TIMES IT IS A PLACE

FOR QUIET RELAXATION. YOUR LIVING ROOM SUMS UP YOUR RELATIONSHIP WITH YOUR PARTNER OR

OTHERS YOU SHARE YOUR HOME WITH BECAUSE IT REVEALS YOUR SELF-IMAGE AND WHETHER THIS

PERCEPTION IS IN KEEPING WITH HOW YOU SEE EACH OTHER. LIKE A GOOD RELATIONSHIP, YOUR LIVING

ROOM SHOULD BE A FLEXIBLE PLACE THAT CHANGES AND GROWS WITH YOU. THE OBJECTS AND COLORS

THAT REFLECT YOU AS INDIVIDUALS EVENTUALLY BLEND TOGETHER TO CREATE A ROOM THAT HAS THE

UNIQUE STYLE OF YOU AS A COUPLE, FAMILY, OR GROUP.

what the living room does for you

THE LIVING ROOM IS THE KEY AREA WHEN CREATING HARMONY IN YOUR HOME. A COMFORTABLE AND ATTRACTIVE LIVING ROOM THAT EXPRESSES YOUR PERSONALITY WILL STRENGTHEN YOUR SELF-IMAGE, ALLOWING YOU TO RELAX AND BE YOURSELF. SO YOUR LIVING ROOM WILL SEND OUT MESSAGES ABOUT YOU AND THE WAY YOU LIVE. IT WILL ALSO INFLUENCE THE WAY YOU INTERACT WITH OTHER PEOPLE.

The living room is both a private and a shared space, so it has many functions. Here you can enjoy your own company, or explore and build friendships with your partner, family, friends, and other homesharers.

The secret of a good living room is flexibility. Sometimes it has to provide you with a place to receive and entertain lots of people, but it must also quickly change into a more relaxed and private space. The best way to make sure your living room meets all your needs is to divide it into two specific areas— one for entertaining and one for relaxing.

The main part of your living space should be a dynamic space that reflects your interests and lifestyle. In this sociable area, you can really express your personality, filling it with objects and colors that reflect your personal taste as well as your lifestyle. It is here that you will entertain your friends and family, listen to music, and watch television with fellow homesharers.

personal space

There are always times when you want to be alone, so your living space should also include an area that is smaller and more enclosed. A snug sitting area provides a place where you feel safe and protected. You can be at ease here and share an intimate chat. Even a small room can offer you the space to do this: a comfortable chair in the corner can give you personal space to read a magazine or enjoy a cup of coffee.

As your living room is the place where you are most likely to receive outsiders, it is here that you display your status to other people. The decor and style of your living room sends out messages about who you are and what you do. Sometimes your actual status in society is far from that which you imagine, and your living room may reflect not who you are, but who you would like to be.

We are constantly bombarded with media role models that pressure us to look, behave, and act in particular ways. This often results in people having unrealistic beliefs and expectations about their home and lifestyle. If

WHAT YOUR LIVING ROOM SAYS ABOUT YOU	
what you see	**what it means**
An interesting mix of furniture and furnishings, with personal objects relating to two different people.	Reveals a home shared by highly individual people with different tastes and interests, where both partners respect each other and have equal status.
A coordinated, stylish, but relaxed interior, which has been well planned and thought out.	Reveals two people with shared interests and taste, who can work well as a team.
A room filled with objects that reflect a specific hobby or interest belonging to one person. For example, lots of CDs or a room full of sports equipment.	Reveals the presence of one person more than the other. It could also show a relationship where one partner is more assertive or dominant.

HOW TO SHARE YOUR LIVING SPACE

1 Recognize the need for all homesharers to be represented and included in the living space—including yourself!

2 Try to encourage a joint sense of responsibility for the planning, creation, and maintenance of your living space.

3 Use your living space. Many households end up spending all their time in the kitchen or their individual bedrooms. Enjoy a sense of community.

4 Don't let the living room be dominated by entertainment equipment, such as a TV. This is a place for communication as well as relaxation.

5 If possible, keep food out of the living space. If you don't have room for a separate eating space, create a designated eating area.

6 Don't be afraid to change the look of the living area from time to time. Remember to include all the members of the household in the process.

the style and contents of your living space has been decorated and designed only to impress your neighbors or work colleagues, you will soon feel uncomfortable in the room and end up spending little time in it. If you do not change your living room to be more in tune with the real you, it could end up being a stressful place and even an area that causes conflict within your relationships.

a balanced room

Your living room not only tells you about your status in the world, but also the status of the individuals within your household. A home where all the occupants play an equal part is very different from one where one person plays a dominant role. Your living room can reveal the state of these relationships, and by enhancing this space you can improve the way you relate to each other.

Living rooms are communal spaces and need to reflect and cater to the tastes of all homesharers— however hairy.

arranging your furniture

THE TYPE AND PLACEMENT OF FURNITURE IN YOUR LIVING ROOM WILL HAVE A DRAMATIC IMPACT ON YOUR RELATIONSHIPS. WELL-PLACED FURNITURE CAN ENHANCE FAMILY AND GROUP RELATIONSHIPS, BUT BADLY ARRANGED FURNITURE CAN HAMPER YOUR SOCIAL AND PERSONAL LIFE.

A living room is a multipurpose room, and for this reason you need to have a very flexible furniture arrangement. Large areas can be divided up into a formal area for entertaining guests and a smaller intimate place where you can spend time with each other or alone (see pages 52–3). For a living room to work well, you need a selection of furniture types to provide you with both comfortable seating as well as more formal areas. Extra chairs are invaluable when you have unexpected visitors or you need a chair for reading, writing, or another specific task. While firm seats provide good back and leg support, they should not be the only chairs in your living room or you will never be able to snuggle up together.

If the seating in a living room is sparse or uncomfortable, you will soon discover that your guests leave early and that you do not

POINTS TO REMEMBER ABOUT FURNITURE LAYOUT

1 Make sure you have enough seating for everyone in your home.

2 Always have a selection of seating options in your living room.

3 To encourage conversation, place sofas close together.

4 Provide a separate chair or area away from the center for more private relaxation.

5 Furniture around the edge of the room creates a feeling of formality and distance.

6 People will feel less comfortable in seats with their back to the door.

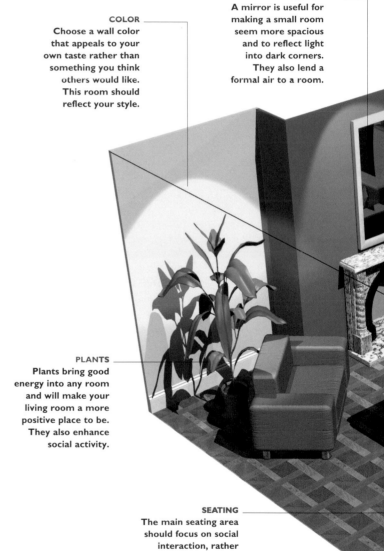

COLOR
Choose a wall color that appeals to your own taste rather than something you think others would like. This room should reflect your style.

MIRROR
A mirror is useful for making a small room seem more spacious and to reflect light into dark corners. They also lend a formal air to a room.

PLANTS
Plants bring good energy into any room and will make your living room a more positive place to be. They also enhance social activity.

SEATING
The main seating area should focus on social interaction, rather than just watching TV. People should be able to talk easily to each other.

FLOORING
You should be able to walk barefoot in your living room, so floors should be warm and pleasant to the touch, preferably made of natural materials.

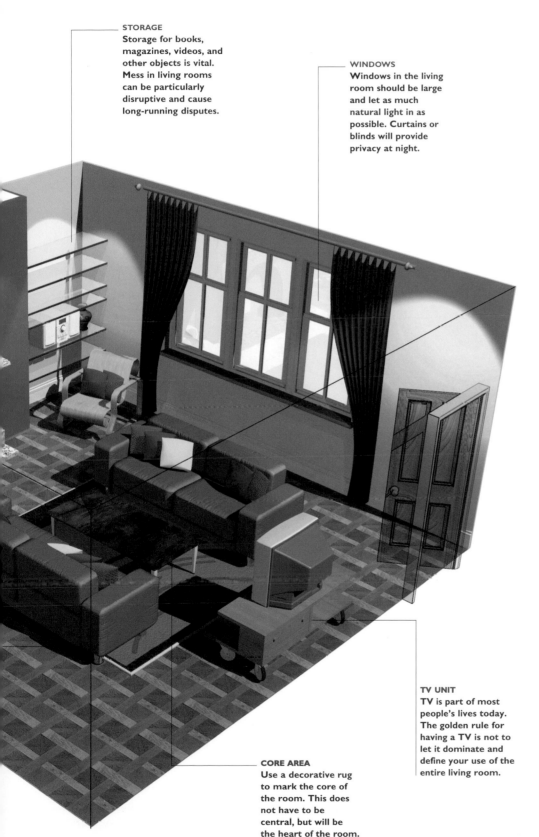

STORAGE
Storage for books, magazines, videos, and other objects is vital. Mess in living rooms can be particularly disruptive and cause long-running disputes.

WINDOWS
Windows in the living room should be large and let as much natural light in as possible. Curtains or blinds will provide privacy at night.

TV UNIT
TV is part of most people's lives today. The golden rule for having a TV is not to let it dominate and define your use of the entire living room.

CORE AREA
Use a decorative rug to mark the core of the room. This does not have to be central, but will be the heart of the room.

spend much time in the room when they are gone. You need to arrange your furniture so people can face each other without having to lean or twist around. Even in a big room, the seating should be fairly close together if you are to avoid shouting at each other. If you place your chairs and sofas too far apart, it will create a more formal use of the room, and people will be less inclined to enter into long, relaxed conversations. Closer seating arrangements, on the other hand, encourage social intimacy and mean you can have a private conversation with ease.

TV tyrant

In some homes, the living room has only one sofa, which often faces the television, leaving no other place to sit. This means that if one person is watching a program, everyone else has to seek refuge elsewhere in the house. While watching a favorite TV program together can be an enjoyable experience good for a relationship, if one person consistently hogs the sofa, his or her partner may look for better company elsewhere.

Living rooms are for living in, so they should be warm and inviting. If you place your furniture around the walls, your place will look like a doctor's waiting room or a passageway. Since ancient times, people have felt most comfortable in circular spaces, and it is easy to create this feeling of security by placing your furniture in a circular arrangement or by introducing a circular rug or coffee table.

Feng shui places a great deal of importance on furniture layout. It stresses the psychological truth that we feel uncomfortable sitting with our back to the door. If you arrange your main seating to face the door, you will naturally feel more relaxed.

color and decoration

WHEN YOU WALK INTO A ROOM, IT IS THE COLOR SCHEME THAT HAS THE MOST IMPACT. THE LONGER YOU STAY IN A ROOM, THE MORE THESE COLORS WILL AFFECT YOUR MOODS AND EMOTIONS, SO YOU NEED TO CHOOSE THE COLORS IN YOUR LIVING ROOM VERY CAREFULLY.

Different colors have different effects on space, making a room appear larger or smaller. Light colors reflect more natural light and make a space appear large and airy. Dark colors have more pigment in the paint, so they make a room more moody and enclosed. Colors in the hot range, such as red, orange, gold, yellow, magenta, and violet, reflect a warm, bright glow that can make a cold room look more cozy and inviting. Cool colors like blue and green are very soothing and can refresh a hot, stuffy room. Not all small rooms need to be white or pastel tones. Small rooms can become vibrant and cozy retreats when colors in rich, warm tones are used.

In order to find the best range of colors, you need to start by looking at the room. The living room itself may suggest the most suitable hues, and you should consider whether your living room is located on the hot or cool side of the house and whether it is a large or small space. You also have to take into account how much sunlight comes into the room and whether the room tends to be hot or cold.

Each color of the spectrum creates a unique signature of moods in humans. Choose a color that will create the right atmosphere for you and your home.

WHITE A white living room creates a sense of space and light and is particularly suited to minimal designs. Off-whites have more warmth than pure white.

GREEN Green is a relaxing color and would create a living room for quiet activities and cozy chats. Other colors can be used with it for warm spots.

YELLOW Bright and positive, yellow is a good living room color for those who want to enjoy social activity and fun.

style and atmosphere

The atmosphere in a room is created primarily by color, so you need to decide what sort of feeling you wish to create. You may want your living room to be relaxing and comforting or perhaps energizing and dramatic.

As this room is closely linked to your identity, a good way of finding inspiration for your living room is to start with a personal object, piece of furniture, or picture that is special to you. Collect several personal or household things that you like and put them together on a tray or coffee table. They could be objects like a necklace, vase, or book cover, anything that reflects the colors and style you like. Put these items together so you can get an idea of the color combinations and style they create.

You could also design your living room color scheme around a shared experience. Perhaps you liked the colors in a place you visited or you wore certain colors on a special occasion. If you use these colors to decorate your living room, you will create an atmosphere that conjures up happy memories for you. This will make sure that you both feel happy and uplifted when you are in the room.

The place where you live is likely to reflect things about your lifestyle as a couple. So you may want to reflect the colors of the landscape and setting of a home inside. The fresh, light colors of the sea and sky look good in beach houses, while country homes lend themselves to richer, more earthy tones.

If you live in an older home or you are a collector of antique furniture, you may like to use colors in keeping with a specific period. You don't have to go way back in history to find a color theme: the colors of the 1950s, 60s, and 70s all have their own flavor, style, and color palette.

EVOKING A MOOD

Color is a powerful means of creating atmosphere and color psychology has been used for many years by commerce and business to alter our mood and behavior. Look at the following list and see how colors can be used to enhance or balance aspects of different rooms.

Neutral or cool colors would suit a bright room and create an inspiring atmosphere.

Rich, deep tones would suit a large, bright room and create an intimate atmosphere.

Light or warm colors would enhance a dark room and create a happy atmosphere.

Warm colors would enhance a cold room and create a happy and inspiring atmosphere.

Warm, rich tones would enhance a large dark room and create an intimate, cozy atmosphere.

Cool or light colors would suit a small hot room and create an airy atmosphere.

RED Full of energy and ideas, red will certainly make for a lively living room. Consider combining it with more calming colors.

BLUE Light blue lifts the spirits and provides a cozy atmosphere. Darker shades may become too gloomy, although chalky tones work well.

PURPLE Purple can be spiritual and sensual at the same time. It produces a secure atmosphere with a hint of creative energy.

lighting

SUNLIGHT CAN BE SEEN AS THE NATURAL POWER SOURCE THAT ENERGIZES AND BRINGS YOUR HOME TO LIFE DURING THE DAY. IT LINKS YOU TO THE CHANGING SEASONS AND RHYTHMS OF THE OUTSIDE WORLD. NATURAL LIGHT MAKES YOUR LIVING ROOM A DYNAMIC AND INSPIRING PLACE. AT NIGHT, OTHER TYPES OF LIGHT TAKE OVER, BRINGING WITH THEM A MORE RELAXED AND RESTFUL FEELING.

In multipurpose rooms like the living room, you need to have a flexible lighting system that makes the most of natural and artificial light. The ideal direction for a living room is southwest in the northern hemisphere and northeast in southern climes. This allows your living areas to benefit from the warmth and light of the sun all day long. If you live in a hot climate, you need to make sure the hot sun does not fade furniture and furnishings, so it is best to put in shutters, blinds, or curtains that can be closed for the hottest part of the day.

The moving quality of the sunlight has powerful mood-enhancing qualities that can help lift depression, balance your emotions, and encourage general well-being. So make the most of nature's free gift and maximize the natural light coming into the room.

MAXIMIZE THE SUNLIGHT

1	Clean your windows well, inside and out.
2	Remove clutter and objects from windowsills.
3	Move dark or heavy furniture away from the front of windows.
4	Replace heavy or dark curtains with lighter colors and sun-filtering fabrics.
5	Change the style of your curtains so they pull well away from the window.
6	Take down valances and swags that may block out the light.
7	Place mirrors opposite windows in small or dark rooms.
8	Hang a crystal pendant in your window to fill your room with rainbows.

LIGHTING UP YOUR RELATIONSHIPS

If you want to:	Try adding:
create a formal atmosphere and promote activity and movement	bright overhead lighting
create a restful and relaxing mood	uplighters or wall washes
create directional lighting for individual tasks; create cozy and intimate spaces	table or side lamps
create a conversation piece and focus	accent lights
create a sense of fun, mystery, intrigue, and focus	lights as art objects

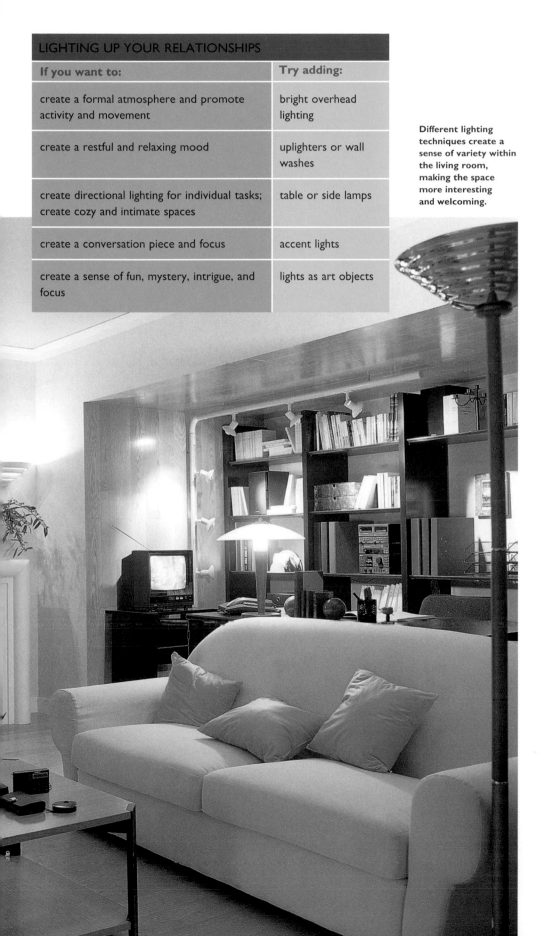

Different lighting techniques create a sense of variety within the living room, making the space more interesting and welcoming.

the practicals

In the winter months and in the evening, your living room requires good light, but it need not be overilluminated. There should be direct light to provide overall illumination as well as background lighting. Good general lighting could be provided by a single, central light, several downlights, or a few wall lights. Reflected light is a softer option and uplighters are designed to reflect light off the ceiling or walls. Unfortunately, they also show up any imperfections in paint- and plasterwork.

A living room also needs directional lighting for tasks such as reading. When switched on, side lamps highlight some areas of your room but leave other parts in darkness. This gives you great flexibility to create occasional intimate spaces within a large room.

creative lighting

Lighting is not only functional and there are many ways to use lighting creatively. Find the right type of light for the right occasion. A fire is a welcoming and heartwarming sight that creates a warm and loving atmosphere. Candlelight is a quick way to change the mood of the room and is very relaxing to the eyes. Small spotlights draw the eye to pictures and you can fit colored filters to spotlights to wash a wall with color.

Lights can also be art objects and enjoyed for their own qualities. A Tiffany lamp with twinkling colored glass can become a focal point in your room while a modern lava, fiber-optic, or bubble lamp adds a sense of fun.

SEE ALSO

CHOOSING COLOR PAGE 22

YOUR CHANGING NEEDS PAGE 24

LIGHT AND COLOR PAGE 150

SOUND THERAPY PAGE 154

ENTRANCE HALL

LIVING ROOM

KITCHEN

BEDROOM

BATHROOM

DISCUSSION

FOCUS

INSPIRATION

INTERACTION

the hearth

THE HEARTH WAS ONCE THE MAIN FOCAL POINT OF THE LIVING ROOM, THE GATHERING PLACE OF THE HOME. IT WAS THE LIVING HEART, PUMPING OUT WARMTH AND SPREADING A FEELING OF WELL-BEING THROUGHOUT THE HOUSE. WE CAN STILL ENJOY THE MAGIC OF THE FIREPLACE TODAY, AND IF YOU HAVE A WELL-USED HEARTH, YOUR HOME WILL ALWAYS BE A NURTURING AND COMFORTABLE PLACE TO BE.

Most traditions have religious celebrations and festivals that involve gathering around and decorating the hearth. In many cultures, too, it is believed that the fireplace has magnetic power that can transform the mood and energy in your home.

How you arrange your furniture around a central point of focus says a lot about your priorities in life. Living flames fulfill a very primary need and have a very special effect on us. As soon as a fire is lit, people gravitate

MARBLE
Marble is a beautiful natural material that comes in many different shades. Most marble fireplaces are found in large, well-proportioned classical buildings, although some designers are installing modern designs using this material. Marble is quite soft and scratches easily and it is not a renewable source, so we should use it with restraint. Marble is cold to touch so a fireplace made of this material will give out a feeling of restraint, coolness, and calmness.

toward its comforting warmth. There is a ritual attached to the setting, lighting, and burning of fuel. The whole experience is therapeutic and is a wonderful way to slow down and release stress. The fireplace is not only healing, but can be a joyful place, too. It often provides a central focus for special occasions such as birthdays, anniversaries, and family gatherings of all types.

A fireplace can be just as dramatic in summer as in winter, whether it is used or not. On a summer evening, place candles on the hearth or mantelpiece and let the warm flickering pervade and soften the atmosphere. Even if you spend an evening watching television, being near your fireplace will help put you in a good mood.

Whatever style of fireplace you choose, it is the perfect place to remind you of the good things in life. The mantel is the perfect place to display a treasured picture, ornament, or candle-stick, and a mirror hung over the mantel creates a moving picture reflecting back the different moods and atmosphere of your room.

heat and light

Today, most homes only use the fireplace as a secondary form of heating. There are many restrictions on the burning of fuel, and if the fireplace is the main source of heating, the most effective way of creating maximum heat output with minimum polluting emissions is to install a high-performance combustion stove in the fireplace. These can work well in most styles of home. Gas fires can provide a good alternative if you do not have a chimney or want to keep cleaning to a minimum. Modern versions include fire baskets filled with pebbles or ceramic stones.

Having an eye-catching hearth in your living room will become a talking point encouraging people to relax and have a good time. However, it is best to choose a fireplace for your home that is in keeping with the architectural style and character of the building.

The type of fireplace and surround you choose will have a particular effect on the energy in your living room. Different materials have their own special qualities that permeate the room and affect the way you use it. Even if your place does not have a chimney, you can often fit a multifuel stove against a wall or place a freestanding type in the center of a large room. A well-designed fireplace or stove can become a sculptural object and a wonderful focal point for the living room and the home itself.

SIMPLY SPACE
A shaped hole in the wall with no surround can be a good choice of fireplace in a small room, where a large fireplace would be too dominant. These help to give a feeling of space and simplicity. They also suit the minimal style—ornate mantelpieces can add an unwelcome touch of period decor that fans of minimalism can't stand. Simple fireplaces also avoid the cost of a mantelpiece.

INGLENOOK
These large, old-fashioned walk-in fireplaces were originally used for cooking as well as heating. They also provided cozy seating areas at the side of the open fire. Inglenooks are best suited to country houses and cottages, and create a strong central focus in a room. They could even be used for their original purpose and include a small oven for baking bread or pizzas. The large size almost creates a room within a room, and this enhances the feeling of closeness and comfort.

VICTORIAN
Attractive period fireplaces are usually made of metal and inlaid with attractively patterned ceramic tiles. The surround and mantel is often made of wood and it was not uncommon to have an overmantel or mirror. Victorian fireplaces have a particularly traditional flavor and suggest a quality of family togetherness that makes them ideal for family homes.

STONE
A stone fireplace is very versatile and can be used in a traditional or modern interior. As stone is difficult to cut and shape, these fireplaces have a natural simplicity that allows you to enjoy the quality of the material itself. Stone has a very solid and honest feeling, creating a room that brings you down to earth. A stone fireplace creates a relaxing mood, especially if you lead a very busy or stressful life and need a haven for relaxation at home.

METAL
Most fireplaces incorporate a metal grate, although metal can be used on its own. Metal stoves come in many shapes and sizes and you can find one to suit almost any style of interior. In contemporary settings a slate, granite, or stone hearth is often combined with metal. Metal has natural magnetism so a metal fireplace can bring different elements of your room together. Some metals are reflective and will mirror the atmosphere in a room back.

windows

WINDOWS ARE PART OF THE ARCHITECTURE OF YOUR HOME AND CAN BE ONE OF THE MOST ATTRACTIVE FEATURES OF A ROOM. AS THE LIVING ROOM IS MEANT TO BE THE MOST USED ROOM IN THE HOUSE, THE WINDOWS SHOULD BE AS LARGE AS POSSIBLE. IF THEY ARE ALSO ATTRACTIVE IN DESIGN, THEY CAN BECOME AN IMPORTANT FOCAL POINT IN THE ROOM.

If you are lucky enough to have a home with a stunning view, a well-placed picture window or door can provide your living room with an external focal point in the day. At night, this large expanse of glass can become a dark void, so you need to be able to cover the windows in order to create a warm and homey atmosphere.

Window treatments play an important part in the overall ambience and atmosphere of a room, and a stunning window dressing becomes a focal point in itself. A window dressing should frame a window and enhance a beautiful view, but it can also serve to hide an ugly or obstructed outlook.

Together with other elements in your living room, the window dressing will help to build up a picture of who you are. Like your clothing, window styles reflect not only your personality and inner space, but also the state of your relationships.

Roman shades made from a light fabric allow light to enter a living room in the day, but will reflect interior lighting back into the room at night. A pointed base makes a pleasing, sculptural finish.

WINDOW DRESSING REMINDERS

VELVET
Fabrics such as velvet or velvet lookalikes add a touch of luxury and dazzle to any living room.

SILK
Silks give a luxurious impression. Their minimal weight gives them a fresher touch than heavier fabrics.

COTTON
Cottons have a fresh, wholesome feel that seems to suggest health and well-being.

BLINDS AND SHADES
These give a contemporary and uncluttered look to a living room, but can be too functional for some.

CURTAINS
Long, flowing curtains are crucial for a traditional-style living room, bringing a sense of formality.

CURTAIN TIEBACK
A curtain tieback creates a sweeping form that makes a pleasing frame for a window.

In the living room, you can tell a lot about the occupants by the type of window dressing they choose. Simple, uncluttered styles reflect relaxed relationships, while frilly and fussy styles can show a more romantic or even sentimental couple. Heavy or ornate styles show a caring and thoughtful relationship when used sympathetically, but if used on small windows, they can show a couple who are concerned with image, not with reality.

less fuss, more light

Today, the trend is for less fussy treatments with headings and poles that are simple in design. Plain curtain styles allow maximum light to enter the room and create an uncluttered backdrop for other features and furnishings in the room. The size of the windows in older homes means they lend themselves to more formal designs, but you can always interpret them in a modern way. Try using cool linens or exotic prints to create a sense of drama. All windows benefit from full-length curtains that create movement.

fabrics

The fabrics you select for your curtains will have a major impact on how you will view and use your living room. Soft, flowing fabrics move gently in the wind and soften the light. They create a quiet and relaxing atmosphere that soothes the mind and spirit.

Bright, colorful cottons are more informal and make a cheerful and happy room perfect for social and family activities. Plain heavier fabrics give an air of sophistication and elegance to a room, while country prints look fresh and romantic. Silks can look extravagant and luxurious, but they also lend themselves to contemporary uncluttered lifestyles.

CHOOSING WINDOW TREATMENTS

If you live in a contemporary-style home, you may want to incorporate the simple lines and functionality of blinds or screens rather than curtains. These reduce the sense of clutter that bulky curtains can create, but can be too restrained for some tastes.

HEAVY CURTAINS

Using a thick, heavy material for your curtains will add a touch of luxury and comfort to the living room. If they are pinned back during the day, they will create pleasing lines of material that also enhance the sense of comfort and effectively frame the view. They work best with tall windows.

WINDOW SHADES

Window shades that roll up are widely used and come in many different colors and finishes. They are plain and functional, which means that they can give your living room a clean and simple look. If you want to make a more intimate living room, it is better to combine them with other forms of window dressing.

VOILES AND LIGHT MATERIALS

As the living room is not for sleeping, it is not necessary to have curtains that block out every particle of light. Light curtains that move in the breeze create a wonderful, airy effect that affect the whole atmosphere of the room. Light curtains suit sunny rooms.

ROMAN SHADES (main picture, left)

Roman shades create a softer look than most other types. They need less fabric than curtains, so you can splash out on something really expensive. This type of shade looks good with stripes, panels, and borders; and you could even block-print the edge yourself. These shades are useful in situations where bulky curtains would get in the way, but they combine well with curtains, too.

BAMBOO AND CANE BLINDS (above)

Bamboo, cane, or paper blinds have wonderful light-filtering properties; and the patterns and shadows they create can enhance a minimal or uncluttered room. They suit sunny rooms because they take the dazzle off direct sunlight while allowing light to enter and illuminate the room.

VENETIAN BLINDS (above)

Venetian blinds can be made of metal, wood, or plastic, and have a more formal look than other types. They are also very functional and give privacy while allowing the maximum light to enter the room. Wooden shutters are a type of blind and can look warm and inviting while remaining uncluttered.

living room moods

YOUR LIVING ROOM SHOULD BE A VIBRANT AND FLEXIBLE SPACE. IT CAN TAKE ON THE COLORS AND FEELINGS OF THE SEASONS, THE DIFFERENT TIMES OF DAY, AND ALSO REFLECT DIFFERENT ASPECTS OF YOU. IT CAN ALSO PROVIDE YOU WITH INSPIRATION AND THE OPPORTUNITY TO INDULGE YOUR CREATIVITY.

The different uses you have for your living room will mean that it has to take on different moods at different times. This can be achieved by creating different spaces within the room and also with clever lighting. Whatever style you decide on, the living room needs to have a focus of attention around which people can gather. This relaxing atmosphere puts you at your ease, and you are much more likely to be able to relax and be yourself.

We all get tied down with habits and rituals that make our lives feel dull and uninteresting. Your living room gives you the opportunity to see your life from a different angle. Even if you love your living room, changing some of the elements from time to time is an empowering act that opens your eyes to new possibilities and opportunities. The regular practice of change can also help you see your relationships in a new and revealing light.

Moving your furniture around brings freshness to your living room. By introducing some inspirational objects, such as a bowl of bright flowers, a cushion, or a colorful lamp, you can add some sparkle that changes your routine and broadens your outlook.

CHANGE YOUR LIVING ROOM, CHANGE YOUR MOOD	
to do this:	**try this:**
uplift and enliven	burn several candles, arrange your cushions diagonally, hang a crystal pendant in a window.
refresh and cleanse	clear up, dust, and vacuum well—open a window or door and let in air and light.
make more relaxing	put tinted bulbs in lamps, play soft music
improve comfort	move furniture closer together and cover your sofa with a soft throw, get a deep pile rug
calm and quiet	float white or blue candles or flowers in a bowl, burn some soothing aromatherapy oils
air of celebration	display flowers with ribbons and exotic fruits, hang bright cards, use silver, gold, and red.
focus and clarity	clear clutter, burn grapefruit or lavender oil, put a single flower in a vase, add something yellow.

Rearranging the area around the hearth is quick and simple, but can have a huge impact on the feel of the living room, renewing its energy and atmosphere.

ENHANCE THE FIRE

FIRE IS THE DOMINANT ENERGY IN A LIVING ROOM, ENHANCING SOCIABILITY, COMMUNICATION, AND EXPRESSION. TRY THESE SIMPLE WAYS TO INCREASE THE FIRE ENERGY AND HELP YOU TO FEEL ENERGIZED WHEN YOU'RE IN YOUR LIVING ROOM.

Move the furniture around to create movement and change in your life.

Have a variety of seating options to make everyone welcome.

Use your fireplace—it creates magnetic energy and brings people together.

Keep the space clear and uncluttered to promote a positive state of mind.

Use colors that express your personality in the furniture and furnishings.

Use sun-filtering curtains or blinds that let the sunshine in.

Place a display of red flowers in the southern corner, to attract good fortune.

Candles will help to bring more fire energy into the living room. If you don't want naked flames in the room, you could also use lights that cast the same color as flames.

SEE ALSO

OUR HOMES, OURSELVES PAGE 10

THE HEALTHY HOME PAGE 14

CHOOSING COLOR PAGE 22

AROMATHERAPY PAGE 152

escape within

STRONG COLORS AND TEXTURES CREATE A VISUAL FEAST, WHILE BOWLS OF FLOWERS AND FRUIT SCENT THE AIR. SENSUAL INTERIORS LIKE THIS REFLECT A RELAXED HOUSEHOLD, CREATING A REVITALIZING ENVIRONMENT FOR RELATIONSHIPS.

LIGHTING

The success of this room lies in its lighting. The natural light and airy interior creates a connection with nature and the outside world. The full-length windows are covered with lightweight sun-filtering curtains. These create a feeling of light and coolness, and bring moving energy into the room. The high ceilings may be welcome during the day, but at night the ceramic lamps bring the stability of the earth element to the room.

Do—Maximize natural light with sun-filtering drapes or blinds.

Do—Keep wall colors light, warm tones that reflect light into the room and keep it cool.

Do—Use Table lamps to make a large space more intimate in the evening.

Do not—Cut out the light with heavy valances and fussy curtains.

Do not—Use pastels if you want to create a hot or exotic atmosphere.

Do not—Light the room just with one central light.

LAYOUT

Large, spacious rooms are a real asset for open-plan living, but they need to be laid out carefully or they become cold, impersonal spaces. In multi-functional rooms arrange your furniture so the room is divided into different areas. Two matching sofas create balance and harmony, and can be placed opposite each other or facing a focal point. By putting the sofa away from the eating area and placing lamp tables at each end, you create a private entertainment space. This dining table is located near the windows, making it perfect for family meals and useful as a work space.

TIPS FOR AN OPEN-PLAN LAYOUT:

• Place sofas close together to create an intimate sitting area.

• Face your living room furniture away from the dining table.

• Use matching lamps and side tables to create a sophisticated relaxation area.

• Arrange your seats to face a strong focal point.

• Put your dining table close to the kitchen.

• In a large space, have both a formal and informal eating area.

DECOR

To create a strong and relaxed atmosphere, you need to be bold in your approach. Flat areas of color create a modern style that allows you to enjoy your room to the full. Use rich colors that remind you of the sights and sounds of an exotic location or somewhere you enjoyed a happy time together. Solid fabrics let you enjoy the effects of the colors more than patterns and contribute to an uncluttered lifestyle and a feeling of honesty in your relationships. If your sofas have removable washable covers, get a second set so you can change them with the seasons. A bowl of aromatic oranges and lemons enhances the tactile and sensual atmosphere, but you could also use some other simple but bold and colorful objects. The high ceilings in this room have been painted a darker tone—not only to create the effect of looking up into the heavens, but also to make the ceiling appear lower, making the room more homey.

DECOR DOS AND DON'TS

Do—Use strong contrasting colors.

Do—Use plain or striped fabrics rather than patterns.

Do—Introduce seasonal changes with bowls of flowers and fruit.

Do not—Use too many bright colors unless you are sure you can live with them without tiring of them.

Do not—Have heavy fabrics or complicated designs on your curtains.

Do not—Include delicate or intricate decorative objects.

party place

THIS ROOM IS BUILT FOR PARTYING. IT KEEPS AS MUCH SPACE FREE AS POSSIBLE BY USING LARGE, STYLISH CUSHIONS AS A FORM OF FLEXIBLE SEATING. THE EXPOSED BRICKWORK AND SPOTLIGHTS BRING A THEATRICAL ELEMENT TO THE ROOM.

WARM LIGHTS

Lighting is used to great effect here to keep the room from looking cold and naked. Try to imagine it with fluorescent lighting—the space would look bare, even hostile. Colored lighting throws splashes of purple onto the seating area and picks up the reds and purples of the flowers. Natural wood flooring provides a warm undertone. Finally, the blazing fire gives the room a warm heart and creates a cozy, romantic atmosphere.

SPACE WITHIN SPACE

Lighting is also used here to create different areas within the one room. A plain, open space can be overpowering and threatening. By picking out distinct areas, intimate new spaces are created.

SHAPE CHANGERS

Spotlights throw light onto the walls in dramatic, random strips. This changes the textures, making the wall more interesting and mysterious.

INDUSTRIAL CHIC

The exposed brick wall and theater-style lighting rack give the space a feeling of fantasy and make-believe. It seems to suggest that anything could happen here, and fantasies can be played out. During the day, natural light will magically transform the space into a refined, minimal space again—until night falls and the dream space is created once more. Although the look is restrained and minimal, there is a sense of luxury and indulgence here. This effect is great for sparking life into your relationship, especially if you enjoy socializing. However, they can be difficult spaces to fill with just two people.

FOR INDUSTRIAL CHIC

- Lots of space for parties.
- Minimal clutter.
- Implication of gleeful decadence.
- Inspiring setting.
- Low maintenance.

AGAINST INDUSTRIAL CHIC

- Can be cold, impersonal spaces.
- Unreal setting can be alienating.
- Large spaces make couples feel alone
- Difficult to heat properly.
- Little space for privacy.

FLEXIBLE SEATING

Having a seating system that invites guests to move around and choose their own place to sit makes a space dynamic and fun. This will ease social interaction, as no one will feel trapped or cornered, but rather can move about as they want. This is a great setting for a lively, uninhibited relationship, in which both partners enjoy socializing. It is also a perfect arrangement for a home that is shared by three or more people.

EASTERN STYLE

The low table and cushions are a modern echo of traditional Chinese and Japanese seating. It literally grounds you, making meals more intimate, but also adding a touch of formality and respect for tradition.

ON THE BENCH

A long wall bench is great way of seating lots of people without taking up too much space. It can also double as a spare bed for guests.

DRAMA AND MYSTERY

This whole space exudes a sense of drama and mystery. The theatrical lights bring out the most flamboyant parts of people's characters, encouraging them to really let go and play a part. The moody lighting also creates an air of intrigue—adding to the excitement of the space. Use this effect in your home if you want to release your creative potential, explore new experiences, and add a bit of personal drama and intrigue.

DRAMA QUEENS

The downside of an effect like this is that it can lead to shallow or avoidant relationships. If we are always having to play a part in this dramatic space, when are we really ourselves?

REALITY BITES

To avoid this possible problem, such a space should be contrasted by other rooms in the home. More down-to-earth styles can be used to create a touch of healthy reality.

open plan

MINIMAL INTERIORS ARE OFTEN PREFERRED BY BUSY WORKING COUPLES WHO ARE SURROUNDED BY NOISE, COLOR, AND ACTIVITY DURING THE DAY. WHEN THEY COME HOME, THEY NEED A COMPLETE CHANGE OF SCENE AND A QUIET SANCTUARY WHERE THEY CAN RELAX AND RECHARGE THEIR BATTERIES.

FOCAL POINTS

In large, open-plan living rooms like this, there can be more than one focal point. The architecture of the room or the space itself can create points of interest. Here the roughly hewn upright wood posts are eyecatching, and the strong lines accentuate the feeling of lightness and space. The wooden floor, which is left uncovered, is also a strong focal point for the room. Although this is a minimally furnished room, the richness of the floor holds your attention so the large space does not feel too impersonal. While the floor and posts are the main focal points in the room, the bowl of lilies add seasonal focus.

TIPS FOR CREATING FOCAL POINTS:

• An architectural feature makes a visual point of interest.

• Natural materials like a wooden floor gives you a tactile focal point.

• A bowl of flowers relaxes and focuses the mind.

• Setting the sofa to one side gives you a better view of the room.

LAYOUT AND FURNITURE

When furnishing and decorating a minimal interior, you have to get down to the bare essentials. Objects and furniture are chosen for their clean lines, and color is reduced to neutral tones. In this interior the occupants have not compromised comfort, and the one sofa is large enough to seat several people, while the soft wool rug defines the relaxation space. While many couples enjoy light, open living rooms, very few people like to sit in the middle of a large room. Placing the sofa where the ceiling is lower creates a sense of security, while giving you the opportunity to enjoy the space. The large palm tree and other potted plants enhance the natural theme and make you feel safe and protected.

MINIMAL LIVING

Pro—Creates a healthy environment that is easy to clean.

Pro—Relaxes the mind and alleviates stress.

Pro—Is functional and simple, so it accommodates your changing moods.

Con—Unless you are both neat, spaces can easily become cluttered.

Con—Minimal interiors can be stark and cold.

Con—Are not child friendly.

LIGHT AND COLOR

If your living room has good natural light, sunlight and shadow will be a strong decorative element in the room. The movement of the sun will give a minimal room movement and life. In this double-volume space, the shadows created by the balustrades enliven and energize the room. In the evening a large space can be cold and even frightening, so you need soft lighting to create a more intimate and warming atmosphere. Here the three simple wall lights allow you to light the seating area separately from the main room.

Most minimal interiors are painted in white. This hue is the nearest to natural sunlight and contains all the other colors of the rainbow, so it has a feeling of wholeness. Brilliant white does not exist in nature, and every white has a warm or cool tone. So when choosing a white decorating scheme, pick a soft off-white to reduce the starkness and glare. Texture like that found in the soft rug will also add interest in an all-white space.

Do—Use off-white tones for natural lightness.
Do—Make the most of sunlight and shadow.
Do—Balance white with warm materials.
Do—Introduce another color to the room.

Do not—Use brilliant white or your room will be cold and uninviting.
Do not—Light the room with one central light.
Do not—Choose white fabrics or furnishings which are not washable.

SEE ALSO ─○
WHERE YOU LIVE PAGE 12 ─○
MINIMALIST OR COZY LIVING? PAGE 20 ─○
CHOOSING COLOR PAGE 22 ─○
LIGHT AND COLOR PAGE 150 ─○

ENTRANCE HALL
LIVING ROOM
KITCHEN
BEDROOM
BATHROOM

DISCUSSION
FOCUS
INSPIRATION
INTERACTION

intimate spaces

FOR BUSY COUPLES, THE EVENING CAN BE THE ONLY TIME OF THE DAY WHEN THEY CAN BE STILL TOGETHER. THIS ELEGANT ROOM IS GIVEN COMPLETELY TO AN ISLAND CREATED BY TWO DAY BEDS. READING LIGHTS AND A CENTRAL TABLE ARE ALL THAT IS NEEDED TO COMPLETE A PERFECT SETTING FOR A QUIET NIGHT IN.

PRIORITIES

By making this intimate area the main focus of the room, the couple who live here are clearly demonstrating that they prioritize their relationship. Visual statements of commitment such as this really have an impact on relationships, additional to benefits of actually using the area to be together. While other rooms in the home need to be more flexible and able to accommodate numerous guests, giving a living area to an area where you can just be together is well worth the loss of space.

DAY BEDS

These two beds are perfect for lounging together in the evening or on the weekend. With cushions at both ends, a couple can sit facing each other and chat while they are reading.

ROOM FOR TWO

The space has been arranged for two people and cannot accommodate more than that comfortably. However, the room is uncluttered, and it would be easy to add a few more chairs if necessary.

LIGHTING AND COLOR

The lighting here is essential to creating a special, central space. There is no central downlighter at all in the room. A bright light is left in the adjoining room to create enough background illumination. Small candles are used around a table of photographs to create a warm spot in the room, away from the central area. Finally, two reading lamps with flexible necks mark the central area itself. The overall effect is one of intimacy and quiet. The focus is on the couple using the space, not the space itself, so everything is used to say that being together is the purpose of this room.

WARM TONE

The walls are a pale shade of terracotta, enhancing the warmth and supportive air of the room. This reflects the warmth of the natural wood flooring. Between them, they create a cozy yet airy room that isn't too stuffy. Terracotta is an earthy color that will help you to focus on and enjoy the present moment together. This shade also has a touch of peach in it, which is particularly good for relationships as it encourages intimacy and sharing. All in all, the colors in this room make it a powerful energy center for relationships.

TEXTURE

Subtle touches add just enough sensual texture to this nurturing room. The white of the coverings on the day beds create a fresh, welcoming impression, while a gray sheepskin rug adds a touch of textural variety. The sculptural plant with its long, green shoots and reflective leaves also brings life and interest into the room. Together with the soft lighting, the texture here is totally in keeping with a space for loving and caring.

ELEGANCE

The whole space works with the architectural style of the home. The traditional moldings, architrave, and baseboard are picked out in white to contrast with the warm color of the walls and ceiling. The rest of the room follows from this foundation, building on elements of restrained style and unspoken elegance and grace.

SEE ALSO

FINDING YOUR STYLE PAGE 18 —○

MINIMALIST OR COZY LIVING? PAGE 20 —○

CHOOSING COLOR   PAGE 22 —○

LIGHT AND COLOR PAGE 150 —○

assess, discuss, and agree

THIS PAGE WILL HELP YOU DISCOVER THE BEST WAY OF IMPROVING YOUR LIVING ROOM. IT MAY BE THAT ALL YOU NEED TO DO IS TO MOVE THE SOFA OR BUY A LAMP. IT MAY TURN OUT THAT A TOTAL MAKEOVER IS THE BEST SOLUTION. BECAUSE THIS IS A SHARED SPACE, IT IS IMPORTANT THAT BOTH PARTNERS AND ANYONE ELSE WHO LIVES IN THE HOME IS INVOLVED IN DISCUSSING AND AGREEING ANY CHANGES.

In order to find out what changes you need to make, you first need to consider how you use and how you feel about your living room as individuals. By focusing on your personal needs, you will also find out how your relationship is reflected and impacted by your living room. In a relationship, we can take our partner for granted—this exercise can really help you to get to know each other again.

Try to answer the following questionnaire honestly and objectively and don't be afraid to express your opinion. The process of discussing and comparing your answers with your partner can help to highlight good and bad points within your relationship.

step one

assess and compare your personal feelings about the way you use the living room

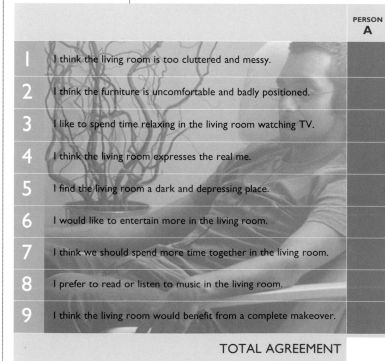

		PERSON A	PERSON B	PERSON C
1	I think the living room is too cluttered and messy.			
2	I think the furniture is uncomfortable and badly positioned.			
3	I like to spend time relaxing in the living room watching TV.			
4	I think the living room expresses the real me.			
5	I find the living room a dark and depressing place.			
6	I would like to entertain more in the living room.			
7	I think we should spend more time together in the living room.			
8	I prefer to read or listen to music in the living room.			
9	I think the living room would benefit from a complete makeover.			
	TOTAL AGREEMENT			

step two

Share your answers. Unless you are totally in tune with each other it is likely that you have different and opposing ideas about some aspects of your living room. The best place to start is to find common ground—discuss aspects that you both think should be changed. This gives you a positive base from which to work.

step three

Discuss your differences. If you have strong and opposing opinions about a particular element of the room, for example the colors, lighting, or furniture layout, accept the fact that neither of you can have exactly what you want. It's much better to find something you are both reasonably happy with rather than for one person to give in to the other. Come to a conclusion about whether you need to improve just some aspects of the room or redecorate the whole space completely.

Discuss and agree whether you have adequate lighting to meet all your needs. Look at the table below to help you make a final decision about what changes you should make.

A COMPLETE LIVING ROOM MAKEOVER

to change:	do this:
clutter	Clear the room completely. Sort through and remove all unnecessary items. Reintroduce objects one by one.
services	Have a professional install the services (TV, telephone, sockets) you need.
lighting	Source different types of lights and select the ones you like.
colors	Decide on your colors—try out some samples on your walls.
furniture	Remove items you do not need and source new furniture required.
layout	Rearrange the furniture.
window dressing	Decide on the style and order your curtains or blinds.
focal point	Install or rearrange your room to create a new focal point.
inspirational items	Hang pictures, display items, add new finishing touches.

WHAT FUNCTIONS DO THE LIGHTS IN YOUR LIVING ROOM PERFORM?

ANSWER THE FOLLOWING QUESTIONS, CHECKING THE LIGHTS THAT YOU HAVE IN YOUR LIVING ROOM:

	Question	Solution
1	Do you have good overall light or do you need to change or add lights?	central, hanging, downlights, spotlights, wall lights
2	Do you have a softer option that still gives good overall light?	uplights, table lamps, floor lamps
3	Do you have a good directional lamp or lights for more exacting tasks or to highlight objects?	floor-standing reading lamp, side table reading lamp, accent lights for pictures
4	Do you have any of the following available to create an air of intimacy, celebration, mystery, or fun?	a working fireplace, candles, unusual lamps or lights

CHAPTER

3

kitchens and dining rooms

PREPARING AND SHARING A MEAL TOGETHER IS THE MOST FUNDAMENTAL WAY WE CAN SHOW OUR AFFECTION FOR EACH OTHER. THE KITCHEN IS A CRUCIAL PART OF THE HOME ON AN EMOTIONAL LEVEL, FOR IT IS THE AREA WHERE WE CAN TAP INTO CREATIVE ENERGY AND DEVELOP OUR NURTURING INSTINCT. RELATIONSHIPS THRIVE WHEN YOUR HOME LIFE REVOLVES AROUND AN ORGANIZED AND HOMEY KITCHEN. WHILE THE KITCHEN CAN BE SEEN AS THE HEART OF THE HOME, THE DINING ROOM IS THE DIGESTIVE CENTER. IN THIS AREA WE NOT ONLY DIGEST OUR FOOD, WE TAKE TIME TO DIGEST LIFE. SOCIAL EXCHANGE AT MEALTIMES DEEPENS BONDS OF FRIENDSHIP AND STRENGTHENS RELATIONSHIPS AND FAMILY TIES.

ENTRANCE HALL
LIVING ROOM
KITCHEN
BEDROOM
BATHROOM

DISCUSSION
FOCUS
INSPIRATION
INTERACTION

relationships and your kitchen and dining room

THE KITCHEN IS THE HEART OF YOUR HOME AND SHOULD SEND OUT WARMING ENERGY TO EVERYONE. NOT ONLY DOES THE KITCHEN OFFER YOU A PLACE TO NURTURE AND FEED YOUR BODY, BUT IT IS A PROTECTED PLACE THAT CAN PROVIDE FOR YOUR EMOTIONAL NEEDS AND COMFORT. IT IS SOMEWHERE THAT SHOULD ATTRACT YOU WHEN YOU NEED A BOOST AND YOU SHOULD LEAVE IT FEELING SATISFIED AND RELAXED.

An open-plan kitchen and dining room often becomes the most popular room of the home. Make sure it suits the needs of all the members of your household.

When you walk into the kitchen and anticipate a delicious meal, you naturally slow down. As you focus on the here and now, your mind relaxes and you become more sensitive to the energy around you. In this state of heightened awareness, it is easy to pick up the atmosphere of a room. If your kitchen is a comfortable place to be, you will pick up good vibrations. The more time you spend here, the more you will absorb the feel-good factor, and the more this will permeate other areas of your life.

It is in the kitchen that you can let down your defenses and have a good laugh and a gossip. Preparing food and sharing healthy, nourishing meals is one of the most humanizing aspects of our lives. If your kitchen is entirely functional, it will reflect the attitude that food is a fuel and less of a pleasurable and sensual experience. It is unlikely that you would want to linger in a completely utilitarian kitchen. A nurturing environment here can help create new bonds and also strengthen ties with your partner, family, and friends.

WHAT KITCHEN AND DINING AREAS SAY ABOUT YOU

YOUR KITCHEN AND EATING AREAS WILL REFLECT HOW CLOSE AND STRONG YOUR EXISTING RELATIONSHIPS ARE AND BY IMPROVING THESE SPACES YOU WILL PROMOTE A RELAXED AND LIVELY FAMILY ATMOSPHERE.

If you have this:	It could mean this:
a little-used kitchen	a couple or homesharers who place little importance on relationships
a little-used dining area	a home where there is little time for relaxing, sharing, and conversation
a dirty or neglected kitchen	people with low self-esteem and lack of self-confidence, a poor attitude to food
a messy kitchen full of clutter	home relationships where no one takes responsibility for their actions
a farmhouse kitchen with table	a household with a relaxed informal and healthy attitude to food
an open-plan kitchen and dining area	a home where there are open and flexible relationships
a high-tech kitchen	an organized couple who may have a clearly defined relationship; but unused gadgets reveal a need to impress and show status
a small but well-planned kitchen	a caring, healthy attitude to each other and food
a large formal dining room	a family where everyone knows their place
no proper dining table in the home	a lack of communication and sharing

WOOD & EARTH ENERGY

- A beautiful table promotes honesty and strength.
- Warm, earthy colors help you to feel nurtured.
- A cozy corner with an armchair brings an air of comfort into the room.
- Natural wood floors and work surfaces create a feeling of warmth.
- A display of fresh fruit and vegetables brings appetizing color and aroma.
- A windowbox of fresh herbs helps to create a healthy, living environment.
- An uncluttered kitchen gives you space to be creative.

the energy of the kitchen

In your kitchen, you can draw on the strength of two great forces, wood and earth energy. The functional aspect of the kitchen relates to wood energy, which is firm and strong but also gives out a feeling of warmth and flexibility. Wood energy helps us to be creative and spontaneous but needs to be balanced by our feminine side, which gives us the capacity to give and receive love. This nurturing aspect of a kitchen is fed by strong earth energy. When you get the right mix, this energy will encourage close friendships and you will experience a new zest for life.

a comfortable dining area

As our feelings of well-being and satisfaction are so closely linked to emotional security, it is natural to want to eat your meals close to the safe haven created in the kitchen. This is why it is traditional to eat in the kitchen—many people prefer to perch on a stool rather than sit at a dining table. The farther we move away from the source of security, the less relaxed we become. In formal dining areas we are much more likely to watch what we say and do. When making and decorating an eating place away from the kitchen, you need to recreate a similarly supportive and comforting environment. A large dining room can be made cozier with good lighting, earthy colors, and natural materials. These give you psychological support and protection, allowing you to be more relaxed and sociable.

THE JOY OF COOKING

Don't think of chopping vegetables or stirring a pot of soup as a chore; instead treat time in the kitchen as a therapeutic experience. Even washing dishes can provide you with a time for thought and reflection, especially if you have designed your kitchen so your sink is in front of a window.

Preparing food is part of the social experience of sharing a meal, giving you the time to relax and unwind before eating. Cooking is a creative and fulfilling activity and can be a feast of sensory stimulation—if you use fresh natural ingredients, you will be exposed to touch, taste, scent, and color in a way you would not normally experience in everyday life.

In many households, one person enjoys cooking more than the other. However, making a meal for a partner can be a way to learn the gift of service and offer time and commitment to someone whom we care about. It is a good idea for both partners to take at least the occasional turn in preparing a meal. If you are both at home at the right time, cook together.

kitchen design and layout

THE PERFECT KITCHEN BALANCES PRACTICALITY AND COMFORT. IT NEEDS TO BE A CREATIVE AND NURTURING PLACE AND ALSO WELL ORGANIZED AND FUNCTIONAL. THE SIZE AND LOCATION OF YOUR KITCHEN WILL HAVE AN IMPACT ON WHETHER IT BECOMES THE SOCIAL CENTER OF YOUR HOME, BUT ITS FUNCTIONALITY AND EFFICIENCY DEPEND MAINLY ON WHERE YOU PLACE THE MAIN APPLIANCES AND STORAGE FACILITIES. MAKING THE KITCHEN EASY TO USE KEEPS THE PRACTICAL SIDE OF LIFE UNDER CONTROL—GIVING YOU MORE TIME AND ENERGY TO ENJOY THE MORE ROMANTIC AND EXCITING SIDE OF RELATIONSHIPS.

Galley kitchens can be used comfortably by only one person at a time and are common in city apartments and mobile homes. A small kitchen can still be an interesting and uplifting place to be as long as you make the most of the space you have.

Create a streamlined kitchen by using built-in units to maximize storage and working space, and put the sink under a window so you can look outside; this helps to create a feeling of spaciousness. If you need to have the units along one side, make sure there is enough work surface between the sink and the stove. Also make sure the oven and the refrigerator are not too close together.

CLEARING THE CLUTTER

These storage ideas may help you to save space:

A hanging rack can release the need for clutter on work surfaces.

A wall-mounted stepladder for pots and pans is fun and practical.

A wine rack can be built into an awkward space.

Simple shelving is a perfect way to display preserves.

Hang up fruit and vegetables in colorful string shopping bags.

Stacking containers allow you to store more in less space.

Clear glass storage containers allow you to see what's inside.

Old-fashioned metal canisters are practical and attractive containers for a selection of coffee and tea.

An open dish rack gives you quick access to plates.

A flip-up table can make an instant eating area.

This open-plan arrangement allows the cook to join in the conversation going on at the table while still devoting space to a functional kitchen.

To create more space in the kitchen, consider putting the refrigerator just outside. A well-placed bistro table at one end of a narrow kitchen means your partner or friends can chat with you while you work.

large or square kitchens

A square kitchen lends itself to the classic cooking triangle. This links the kitchen's main centers—the stove, sink, and fridge—in a triangle shape to give you maximum ease of use. In a large enough kitchen, place two of

THREE WAYS TO FREE THE COOK FROM SOCIAL ISOLATION

Relationship problems can arise when one person has to cook every day, making that person feel undervalued or resentful of his or her partner, family, or homesharers. Making sure that the kitchen is not entirely cut off from the rest of the house goes a long way to make sure the cook stays in a good mood.

1 Incorporate the kitchen into an open-plan layout with other social areas by making openings and servicing hatches.

2 Create a sitting and eating area in the kitchen by incorporating a breakfast bar, a table and chairs, or a folding wall table.

3 If your kitchen is a separate room, make sure the cook has access to a tabletop television, radio, and hi-fi speakers, phone, and cookbooks.

the centers on one side of the room and the third on the opposite side; in a smaller area, place each center on a different wall. There should be a maximum of two double-arm spans between any two centers. A center island is a good way to reduce the distance you have to walk in a very large kitchen.

In a large kitchen, you have the space to incorporate both built-in and freestanding units. Built-in units are efficient and practical, but individual pieces add personality to the room. A table placed in the center of a kitchen helps to make the whole space a

more friendly and sociable place to be; if the room is L-shaped, a breakfast bar can be used to link the two distinct areas of the room, both functionally and visually.

open-plan kitchens

Open-plan living gives maximum flexibility and a feeling of openness and connection with all parts of the house. You don't have to be living in a specially designed home to give an open-plan feel to your kitchen.

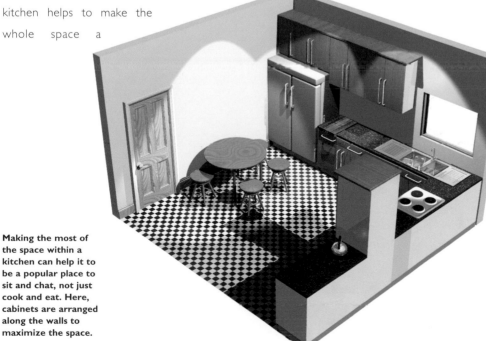

Making the most of the space within a kitchen can help it to be a popular place to sit and chat, not just cook and eat. Here, cabinets are arranged along the walls to maximize the space.

It is never enjoyable to cook in a small enclosed space, so if you have a small kitchen, consider opening it up into your living or dining area. You could do this by incorporating an internal window or by making a half-wall between the two areas. A breakfast bar or large serving hatch means the cook can communicate with people in the living room.

If the space is large enough, try to incorporate an informal eating area in your kitchen (see pages 76–7). Eating together in the kitchen creates a relaxed and informal place for you to share a meal and conversation. A table in the kitchen is also useful because it allows you to sit down out of the way, when others are using the counters or stove.

easy-access storage

Mealtimes can be a headache when you are tired or in a hurry. An organized kitchen will make it a little easier to prepare a meal without the extra frustration of searching for the tools you need. Store items near where they are most likely to be used; for example, keep knives close to the work surface, and pots and pans near the stove and oven.

Items that you use every day should be stored in places that are quick and easy to reach, while other, less frequently used items like vases or special serving dishes can be stored high up or at the back of cupboards. Some kitchen equipment such as toasters and coffee machines may need to be left out; other gadgets should be stored away.

— ENTRANCE HALL

— LIVING ROOM

KITCHEN

— BEDROOM

— BATHROOM

— DISCUSSION

FOCUS

— INSPIRATION

— INTERACTION

color and style

NO MATTER HOW CAREFULLY YOU PLAN AND LAY OUT YOUR KITCHEN, THE ATMOSPHERE WILL DEPEND ON COLOR AND DECORATION. KITCHENS ARE BUSY PLACES THAT SHOULD ALSO HAVE A FEEL-GOOD FACTOR. THE BEST WAY TO ACHIEVE THIS IS BY USING RELAXING COLORS AND A VARIETY OF LIGHTING.

Before you can decide on the right colors and materials for your kitchen, you need to decide on the style and type of atmosphere you wish to create. Ask yourself whether you would like your kitchen to be:

SIMPLE AND STYLISH

A CREATIVE HAVEN

AN EARTHY COUNTRY RETREAT

A RELAXED ACTIVITY CENTER

simple and stylish

By putting in matching cupboards, hiding clutter, and using color and materials to unify the look of your kitchen, you will give the room a sense of calmness. Lighting is also important in creating a spacious atmosphere. To create a feeling of unity, keep the design of your cupboards simple. Choose harmonizing tones of just one or two colors so that no one area of the kitchen stands out. Use soft, light colors to create a sleek appearance and natural materials on the floor and work surfaces.

a creative haven

A creative kitchen needs to be both functional and friendly. A good combination would be to use warm natural colors on the floor or cabinets with slate gray or terracotta on the floor. Contrast these colors with soft color-washed walls. Stainless steel is a good choice for equipment; it is durable and will bring a modern design element into the room. A long, uninterrupted work surface in laminated wood or granite would give you plenty of room to move, and both these materials have a natural glow and beauty.

CHECKLIST FOR A SIMPLE, STYLISH KITCHEN

1	Keep work surfaces free of clutter.
2	Choose tones of one color and another for contrast.
3	Don't let any one part of the kitchen stand out from the rest.
4	Keep the floor and cabinets a similar color.
5	Select matching kitchen equipment, gadgets, and utensils.
6	Good overall lighting helps unify the room.
7	Choose smooth, natural materials for their texture and color.

CHECKLIST FOR A CREATIVE KITCHEN

1	Mix old-style objects with new-style equipment.
2	Use a mixture of warm, earthy colors and contrasting natural shades.
3	Don't worry if something doesn't match as long as it is useful.
4	Display bowls of colorful fruit and vegetables.
5	Wooden cabinets and chopping boards are warm and aromatic.
6	Granite or laminated counters are easy to clean and hard-wearing.
7	Wood, terracotta, or linoleum flooring is warmer.

a relaxed activity center

For most people, the most important thing about the kitchen is not whether it is hard-wearing or clean, but whether they like to spend time there. A kitchen activity center can be decorated in any style, as long as it is light, bright, and comfortable.

The most important way of getting the most from your kitchen is to have somewhere to sit. A table and chairs are ideal, but in a small space a chair or bar stool would encourage your partner or friend to linger while you cook. If your kitchen is large enough, it could incorporate comfortable armchairs and a television at one end. A cheerful rug and some pictures would also change the kitchen into a living area. A fireplace is a natural crowd-puller: a cream, red, or green stove or range can have the same effect. Green gives a fresh, country feel and is good for tiles, cabinets, or fabric furnishings.

If you decide on a simpler, less cluttered look for the decoration, you can quickly change the mood with the addition of a bowl of flowers, fruit, or colored china.

earthy country retreat

Country kitchens have that special, rich, lived-in feel to them that we associate with older-style homes. In traditional country homes, most kitchens contained old-fashioned ranges, sinks, and a mix of freestanding furniture and cupboards. The kitchens were filled with practical objects like baskets, kettles, and pitchers. Hanging racks with hooks were popular for storing pots, utensils, herbs, and strings of onions and garlic.

You can create a rustic mood with "dragged" or "distressed" painted cabinets. Choose blue-gray and earthy green to complement rich wooden counters. Bright colored tiles in rich green, orange, or blue create a striking effect, especially when you mix several colors together. Translucent glazes have a jewellike quality and change in different lighting conditions. Flooring in a country kitchen should look earthy and hand-crafted. Terracotta tiles, stone, or slate are natural materials that look good in a farmhouse kitchen. These can be cold: You may need to add rugs. Wood flooring is a warmer option.

CHECKLIST FOR A RELAXED KITCHEN CENTER

1. Make sure there is a comfortable place to sit.
2. A fireplace, range, or colored stove gives the kitchen a heart.
3. Warm, fiery colors draw people in.
4. Use neutral or natural tones in a light, bright room.
5. A collection of recipe books adds color and interest.
6. A telephone and TV should be placed out of the cooking area.
7. A rug can turn a kitchen into a comfortable room.
8. Arrange the room so the cook can chat and cook.

CHECKLIST FOR AN EARTHY COUNTRY RETREAT

1. Use freestanding pieces and a rustic kitchen table as a centerpiece.
2. Use warm earthy colors for flooring and work surfaces.
3. Paint, drag, or distress cabinets in cream, pale blue, or green.
4. Display earthenware jugs, jars, and dishes in yellow, cream, or blue.
5. Stimulate the senses with displays of herbs and fresh produce.
6. Hand-baked tiles provide a rich, warm texture.
7. Hanging lamps and wall lights look authentic and give flexible lighting options.
8. Woven checked or floral tablecloths, cushions, and window shades.

ENTRANCE HALL
LIVING ROOM
KITCHEN
BEDROOM
BATHROOM

DISCUSSION
FOCUS
INSPIRATION
INTERACTION

sharing your kitchen

THE KITCHEN SHOULD BE A PLACE FOR ENJOYING A SENSE OF COMMUNITY WITH OTHER HOMESHARERS. HOWEVER, IT CAN TURN INTO A BATTLEGROUND IF A FEW SIMPLE STEPS ARE NOT TAKEN TO MAKE SURE HARMONY REIGNS. CATCHING PROBLEMS EARLY WILL HELP AVOID SPILLED MILK.

Sharing your home with lodgers or others with whom you are not closely connected is not easy. It is the state and use of the kitchen that may be most likely to cause you to fall out. To avoid conflict, you need to plan the layout well and give everyone enough cupboard space for their own food items. Knowing which items belong to whom goes a long way in insuring your favorite food is there when you get home. To personalize your storage space, paint your individual cupboard a different color, or if you want to keep the kitchen cabinets matching, stick colored cards or labels on the doors.

Always share kitchen chores and the buying of basic cooking and cleaning products. It

TIPS FOR SHARING YOUR KITCHEN	
1	Avoid friction by having separate cupboards (lockable).
2	Give each person a different shelf in the fridge.
3	Split the bills for shared items.
4	Take turns shopping for basics, or get a regular home delivery.
5	Share a meal every week or have a monthly gathering.
6	Have your own tea- and coffee-making kit in your bedroom.
7	Get a pinboard and attach a roster for household chores.

is a sad fact that no matter how well-intentioned your homemates are, when it comes to clearing up and buying the basics, they soon fall short of your expectations. In a shared kitchen, you need to enforce a routine and make sure everyone sticks to it. A noticeboard is an essential item that can help prevent any misunderstandings if you display a daily and weekly roster of duties and chores. Sharing should not feel like a punishment, so arrange evenings when each person has the exclusive use of the kitchen so they can entertain their own friends.

Everyone who lives in your home becomes part of the family, so having a regular meal together can create a happy atmosphere and cement friendships. Take turns shopping, preparing, and cooking the meal. A good way to make a meal together is to give each person one course to prepare.

KITCHEN SAFETY	
1	Put a short cord on the coffeemaker so it can't be pulled away from the work surface.
2	Get a stove that has a closing lid to keep animals and children off.
3	Keep dangerous cleaning agents in a locked or top cupboard.
4	Keep knives in a lockable drawer.
5	Store food that kids use on a low shelf in the fridge.
6	When cooking, make sure the handles of your pots do not overhang the burners.

sharing your kitchen with kids

Children love food, and for them the kitchen is a magical kingdom full of surprises and delights. Most children are fed in the kitchen, and even when they aren't eating, they are likely to spend lots of time watching and being around adults who are cooking. Children learn from adults, so the way you treat and use your kitchen will quickly be picked up and copied by the younger generation.

Kitchen life should be rich, a hive of activity and creativity. If a child has happy memories related to the kitchen and eating with the family, this positive response will remain with them for life. Involving children in the preparation and cooking of meals not only teaches them an important skill but makes them feel an important family member. Most accidents in the home happen in the kitchen, so you must keep in mind that a kitchen can be a dangerous place for kids.

If your children spend time in the kitchen, you need to provide them with comfortable seating. Young infants should have a high-chair, and a child seat would enable a growing toddler to eat at the kitchen table. A breakfast bar is a good addition for older children. Children don't just use the kitchen for eating; they may use it as a place to play or do their homework or chat to friends. If your kitchen is well planned and an enjoyable place to be, your children can come and go and still leave room for you to work without stress.

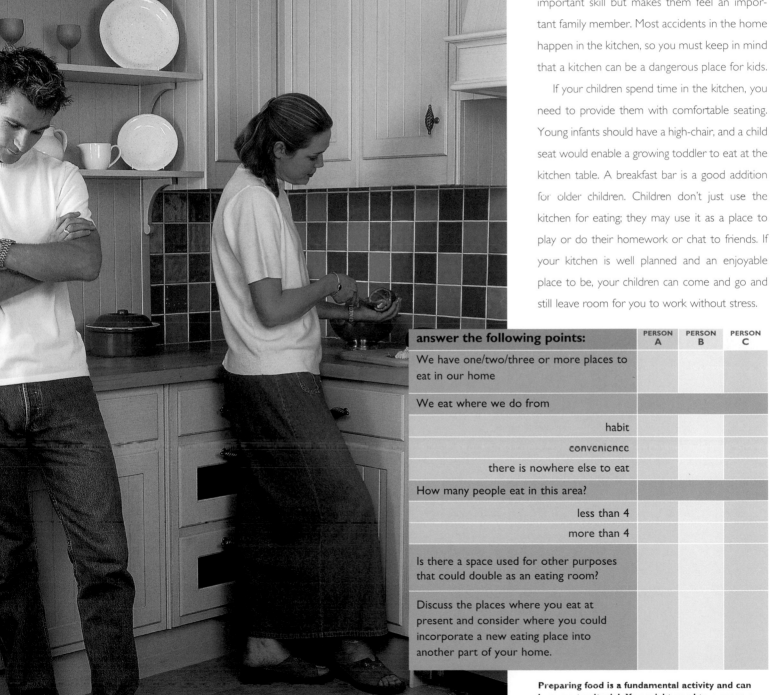

answer the following points:	PERSON A	PERSON B	PERSON C
We have one/two/three or more places to eat in our home			
We eat where we do from			
habit			
convenience			
there is nowhere else to eat			
How many people eat in this area?			
less than 4			
more than 4			
Is there a space used for other purposes that could double as an eating room?			
Discuss the places where you eat at present and consider where you could incorporate a new eating place into another part of your home.			

Preparing food is a fundamental activity and can become territorial. You might need to arrange a timetable to avoid friction in the kitchen.

—●— ENTRANCE HALL
—●— LIVING ROOM
—●— KITCHEN
—●— BEDROOM
—●— BATHROOM

—●— DISCUSSION
—●— FOCUS
—●— INSPIRATION
—●— INTERACTION

dining areas

IT'S VITAL THAT YOU TAKE TIME TO SIT DOWN AND SHARE FOOD WITH THE PEOPLE WITH WHOM YOU LIVE. IF THERE IS NO PARTICULAR PLACE IN THE HOME FOR PEOPLE TO SIT DOWN TO A MEAL TOGETHER, EVERYONE WILL DO THEIR OWN THING. PEOPLE WHO CONSTANTLY EAT TV MEALS OR WALK AROUND WITH SNACKS IN THEIR HANDS HAVE LITTLE CHANCE TO RELAX AND BE SOCIABLE. UNCOMFORTABLE EATING PLACES ENCOURAGE YOU TO EAT FAST—THE QUICKER YOU FILL YOUR MOUTH, THE LESS YOU CAN SPEAK, AND IF THIS BECOMES A HABIT, YOU CAN LOSE THE ABILITY AND DESIRE TO TALK TO YOUR PARTNER OR FAMILY.

If you don't have space for a separate dining room, you should dedicate an area in your kitchen or living room to eating. Even if you have a dining room, it is also useful to have smaller, more intimate eating spaces. Dining rooms end up being the least used rooms in the home because they are often formal rooms that don't suit the occupants' lifestyles.

creating intimacy

We prefer eating in small intimate spaces than in large open areas—visit any cafe or restaurant, and you will notice that the tables by the walls are always filled first. This is because in order to relax and enjoy our food, we need to feel comfortable and emotionally secure. We have an instinctive desire to sit with our back to the wall when we eat, so no one can surprise us from behind.

If your dining area is large or part of an open-plan living area, it is a good idea to separate the area so it feels more protected and comforting. You could use a half-wall or bar unit to divide the space—this works well if you can put your table next to a window or some patio doors. You can also differentiate between the cooking and dining area by using floor tiles in the kitchen and carpeting in the dining space. Another subtle way to divide up a large room is to vary the color scheme

slightly in different parts of the room or to highlight the eating area with accent lighting. Alternatively, you can use a beautiful screen to partition the room. For a more permanent solution, the living and dining areas of an open-plan room can be divided with sliding or folding doors.

occasional eating places

Eating in a different area of your home from usual can help you to see your life from a different angle and help to create a mood of new interest. Many homes offer unexpected places and corners for eating—particularly for meals for one or two. In an older house, a large hall or landing can create a special place for a meal. Even a recess under a staircase can

GUIDE TO INFORMAL EATING

If your main eating area is in or close to the kitchen, dining is likely to be a relaxed and informal affair. Family and friends naturally congregate close by for a drink and a chat while the meal is being prepared. This type of eating arrangement involves everyone. While you are waiting and watching the cook, you will be enjoying the pleasant aromas and feasting your eyes on the bright colors and rich textures around you. These sensory delights help build up a sense of anticipation that contributes to your enjoyment of the meal. If you entertain in the kitchen, you can always give the table a more formal look by using a good-quality tablecloth, your best plates, flowers, and candles.

become a cozy eating nook for one or two. Many of these eating places are oddly shaped, so a drop-leaf or extending table is often invaluable—folding chairs or stools that can be neatly stored in a nearby cupboard when not in use are also handy. Eating in a conservatory or sunroom can also be a special treat, as you can enjoy the light and warmth of the sun when the air is still cold.

Involving or at least considering everyone in the plan for your eating spaces will help you to make sure that they suit all the members of the home and are well used.

INFORMAL EATING

Informal eating has become very popular, but it also means that you may be eating in a large open room or your kitchen clutter will be on view. This is not conducive to creating an atmosphere of relaxation or intimacy. These simple ideas will help you to enjoy eating informally:

1 In an open kitchen/diner, prepare food in advance and leave time to clear up.

2 Dress up a kitchen table for a special meal with a good-quality cloth, flowers, and candles.

3 When eating in the kitchen, dim the kitchen lights and use the task lighting under the cabinets.

4 If you have a kitchen/diner, use dimmer switches to create an intimate atmosphere, and any clutter will also be hidden.

5 Use an L-shaped cabinet or breakfast bar to separate the kitchen and dining areas

6 In an open-plan room change the color scheme or floor-covering in the dining area.

7 Place a table and build window seats into a bay window.

8 Put your dining table near patio doors or a large window.

WHERE CAN YOU EAT?

Assess your home for alternative places to eat. Perhaps you have a study, playroom, or living room that could double as an eating room. Playrooms that have been outgrown can often be converted into dining areas, or your spare room might offer the opportunity for a calm place that you can devote to food. Don't forget outdoor spaces. A patio, terrace, or garden room all make excellent eating areas. Sitting among greenery helps bring the outside into your home and brings a feeling of well-being.

SEE ALSO

OUR HOMES, OURSELVES PAGE 10 —○

FINDING YOUR STYLE PAGE 18 —○

YOUR CHANGING NEEDS PAGE 24 —○

SHARING A HOME PAGE 28 —○

ENTRANCE HALL
LIVING ROOM
KITCHEN
BEDROOM
BATHROOM

DISCUSSION
FOCUS
INSPIRATION
INTERACTION

dining rooms

DINING ROOMS CREATE A WONDERFUL SETTING FOR FAMILY MEALS AND FOR ENTERTAINING. THEY OFFER A CLEAR AND COMFORTABLE SPACE THAT IS DEVOID OF DISTRACTIONS SO YOU CAN CONCENTRATE ON THE RITUAL OF THE MEAL, ALLOWING THE FOOD AND EACH OTHER TO BECOME YOUR FOCAL POINTS.

The best location for a dining room is close to the kitchen, preferably on the same floor and level. If your kitchen and dining room are adjoining rooms, it also makes it easier to serve and clear dishes. A formal dining room that is used mainly at night could easily be located farther away from the kitchen and on the cooler side of the house.

Dining rooms are not only for formal evening meals, they should also be relaxing places that you can enjoy at any time of day. A sunny dining room can easily double as a study or music room during the day. An attractive bureau or folding office unit that can be closed when you have finished your work will help to prevent clutter from spreading onto the dining table and spoiling the room. The presence of a piano can also enhance the ambience of a room during a meal.

Apart from the meal itself, lighting is the one thing that can really affect your enjoyment of a meal. You need to see the food clearly but not to feel you are sitting under a floodlight. Bright light can put us off our food so turn off overhead lights and use wall or table lamps to give your dining area a softer glow. A candelabra hung low over a dining table can provide a dramatic focus point and will create a magical atmosphere. Candlelight is very flattering and gives your table a festive or romantic air.

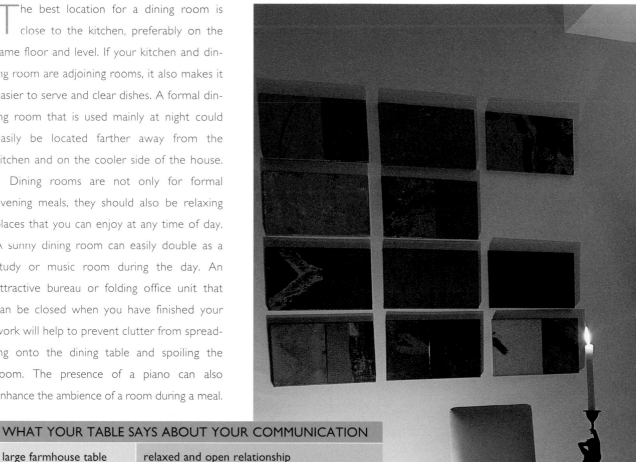

WHAT YOUR TABLE SAYS ABOUT YOUR COMMUNICATION

large farmhouse table	relaxed and open relationship with lots of sharing
small round or oval table	intimate and sincere and caring relationship, equal give and take
cluttered or messy dining table	difficulty in expressing your feelings, lots of things left unsaid
folding table	speaking your mind only when you have to and having difficulty seeing your partner's point of view
low dining table	strong tactile and deep relationships, building relationships

color

Color has a profound effect on our digestion and affects our enjoyment of eating. When we look at a bright red apple or shiny orange, we begin to salivate—these colors actually stimulate our appetite. We also naturally feel

relaxed and comfortable surrounded by warm peach, apricot, and yellow tones. These colors give us emotional support, so we feel safe and are more open to conversation. These colors not only create a bright and uplifting dining area, they will help to improve your sociability levels and ease of communication.

Dark, rich colors are particularly suitable for a traditional dining room used mostly at night. These tones make a large room appear more intimate, and candlelight can make dark walls appear to glow. Dining rooms are often located on the cold side of the house and benefit from rich, warm colors like deep red, burnt orange, or golden-yellow. A glaze or eggshell paint will glow in the evening and look warm and inspirational by day.

Hot colors may not suit your needs. If you lead a hectic or stressful lifestyle, a more restrained color palette for the dining area may be more suitable. Eating can be a quiet and contemplative time, something one may do in silence or on your own. Warm dove gray, rich brown, and tan will have a calming and relaxing effect. When you need to be more sociable, liven up a neutral color scheme with flowers, a colorful display of fruit or vegetables, or use vibrantly colored tablecloths, table mats, napkins, and dishes.

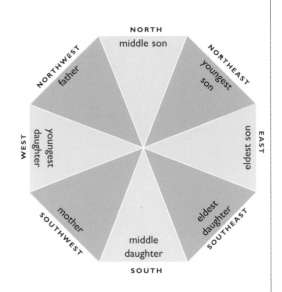

In feng shui, the places around the table are organized according to the compass points.

Dining tables reflect and impact relationships. If your home has no proper dining table or if your table is permanently covered with clutter, it will reflect a scattered home life that lacks cohesion and social interaction.

If your dining table is large, it shows a household where communication is important. Your dining table will also offer you the chance to entertain your family and friends. By increasing the size of your table, you will be more likely to invite more people around for a meal and so improve your social life.

TABLE FENG SHUI

Table shapes, like room shapes, should be regular and give a feeling of wholeness. Good shapes for table are squares, circles, ovals, or rectangles—provided they are not too long.

Unlucky shapes are long narrow tables and tables with cut off corners, which allow good energy to drain away. A true octagonal shape (even though it has corners cut off) is very auspicious.

A square table offers an equal place for four sitters. It can also be fitted snugly into the corner of a room.

Round tables are excellent for promoting communication and equality between homesharers.

The curve on this table helps to reduce the negative aspects of a rectangular table. If you share your meals with homesharers, try to vary your places at a rectangular table.

kitchens for cooking

EVERYONE WHO LOVES FOOD LOVES A COOK'S KITCHEN. WHETHER IT'S A SIMPLE BREAKFAST OR AN EXOTIC DINNER, A WELL-PLANNED KITCHEN IS A JOY TO WORK IN. YOU NEED EVERYTHING CLOSE AT HAND: A SMALL, ORGANIZED SPACE IS MORE PRACTICAL THAN A HUGE ROOM.

DESIGN AND LAYOUT

This kitchen with its double oven and extensive preparation area reflects a household that takes food seriously. The space is arranged so there is a smooth flow between the preparation, storage, cooking, and sink areas. There are plenty of work surfaces, and the mobile butcher's block provides extra preparation and storage space. The choice of design is simple, and the materials reflect a desire to create a homey feel.

TIPS FOR LAYOUT:

• Have essential utensils and cookware close at hand.
• Minimize clutter on the work surfaces.
• A mobile butcher's block can provide extra storage and work space.
• Make sure you have ample work surfaces on each side of your stove.
• A sink near the preparation area cuts down on spillage.
• A large extractor fan reduces odors in an open-plan kitchen.

DECOR

Cooking can be a colorful and sensual affair that can really pep up your interest in life and your relationship. Fresh, natural foods have a wealth of color, texture, and aroma that stimulate not only your appetite, but also your creativity. Most serious cooks concentrate on what they are doing so the less distracting the decor, the better. In this kitchen color is kept to a minimum. The dark tiles minimize the glare and provide a calming backdrop while you work. The stainless steel oven splash

protector, extractor, and refrigerator work together to counteract the heat from cooking and are easy to clean.

TIPS FOR PROFESSIONAL KITCHEN DECOR:

• Flamboyant cooks like bright colors.
• Serious cooks prefer neutral tones.
• If you like old-fashioned cooking, tiles are more country style.
• Metal surfaces are a better choice for exacting modern cooks.
• Wooden surfaces make a kitchen look less cold and industrial.

COLOR AND LIGHTING

Modern kitchens can become very cold and utilitarian if they are not properly lit and softened with some warm colors and materials. The natural beauty of the wooden countertops in this room bring out the natural flavor and aroma of food chopped on them, while still looking good when the kitchen is not in use. This kitchen area is flooded with natural light that makes the functional appearance look less intimidating, so even novice cooks will be encouraged to practice their skills. The household will be more likely to use a multifunctional room during the day if it is light and airy, but make sure you have some good task lighting over the kitchen work areas in the evening.

TIPS:

• Light-toned kitchen cabinets are easier to clean.

• Solid colors are less distracting than patterns.

• Metal finishes keep a working kitchen cool.

Do not—Mix too many colors and finishes.

Do not—Rely on one light source for the whole room.

Do not—Serve a special meal without lighting candles and turning off task lights.

ENTRANCE HALL
LIVING ROOM
KITCHEN
BEDROOM
BATHROOM

DISCUSSION
FOCUS
INSPIRATION
INTERACTION

eating spaces

EATING AREAS LEND THEMSELVES TO ATMOSPHERIC DECOR, RICH COLORS, AND DRAMATIC LIGHTING. THIS DINING NOOK USES ALL THESE TO BECOME BOTH SENSUAL AND INVITING.

LIGHT AND COLOR

It is in your dining room that you can really go to town and use colors you would not dare to use in the rest of your place. The deep-red walls of this dining room glow in the candlelight, giving the room a warm, sensual atmosphere. The main walls are contrasted by a rich blue in the alcove, preventing the room from becoming too oppressive. Fire colors stimulate the appetite and also help you relax and let the conversation flow. Deep red, orange, and gold look good in the day, especially if the room is on the cold side of the house. When not used for dining, this decor would be a good place to curl up with a book or chat on the phone. The two different light sources make this room versatile. The lighting in the alcove lets you see what you are eating even when the main light is turned off.

Do—Choose rich colors to create a cozy, relaxed atmosphere.

Do—Contrast warm with cool hues to prevent the room from becoming too oppressive.

Do—Use dramatic lighting to create an intimate ambience.

Do not—Use neutrals unless you want your guests to leave early.

Do not—Have a bright light on during a meal as it stifles conversation.

Do not—Use dark or muddy colors like olive or navy, which ruin your appetite.

FURNITURE AND LAYOUT

When we are surrounded by natural materials like wood, we feel relaxed and secure, making it the perfect environment to enjoy a meal. Rustic wooden furniture is the perfect choice for an informal family eating area, but sometimes you want to introduce some sophistication into your home. Close-knit families often pride themselves on their beautiful dining tables, and if you have a well-made and proportioned dining table, it is hard to resist sitting down to share a meal with your partner, family, and friends. Even when there are just two of you, a darker-colored table will not appear so big and formal, especially if you have your meal by candlelight. Every meal, no matter how simple, can be made special in this elegant setting.

TIPS FOR LAYOUT:

- Avoid having your back to the door while you eat.
- Keep chairs close so you don't have to shout.
- Polished wood is timeless and elegant.
- Special objects and artwork in your dining room will make it more personal.

classic kitchen

THIS CLASSIC KITCHEN LAYOUT MAKES MAXIMUM USE OF LIMITED SPACE. COUNTERS ALONG THREE WALLS MEAN THAT THERE IS PLENTY OF WORK SURFACE, WHILE THE MAIN APPLIANCES ARE CAREFULLY SPACED AROUND THE ROOM.

MAXIMUM STORAGE

In a small space, storage becomes a key issue for a kitchen. On one hand, it is crucial that you have everything you need close at hand, on the other, it is equally important that the work surfaces are kept clear and free of clutter. In this kitchen, cabinets have been put in wherever there is space for them. This helps to provide enough room for dishes and cooking equipment.

STORAGE FOR COLOR

The storage does not stop with just the cabinets. A high shelf with a hanging bar provides an easy-to-access place for storing various cooking utensils. The stainless steel objects also bring a touch of modern style to the otherwise traditional kitchen decor. Colored containers of all shapes, sizes, and colors are dotted around the kitchen, providing both storage and interest.

LAYOUT

This kitchen follows the classic triangular arrangement for the principal work stations. The stove is placed along one wall, the sink is at 90 degrees to that, and the fridge (not visible in this picture) is placed on the wall opposite the stove. This is the best layout for ease of movement between each of the stations. There is also plenty of surrounding work surface so two people could work here comfortably, efficiently and without getting in each other's way.

A SINK WITH A VIEW

The best place for the sink is against a window. This allows you to gaze out at what is going on outside while you are doing the dishes. The position of the window in relation to the stove also means it is well illuminated—making cooking easier and safer. Cooking with your back to the window casts a shadow over what you are doing. It is also a good idea to avoid putting the fridge and the oven too close together.

LIGHTING

The broad window here takes up almost all of the far wall. This allows as much light into the room as possible and also means there is plenty of ventilation to prevent the kitchen from getting too steamy or smoky. For cooking in the evening, downlighters (not visible) provide adequate lighting to help the cook, while still creating a warm, welcoming atmosphere. The light-colored walls help to reflect light into the various nooks and corners of the room.

Do Have a mixture of task lighting and atmospheric lighting.

Do—Make maximum use of natural light by putting in a large window.

Do—Place the window so it throws light onto the work surfaces.

Do not—Have a single ceiling light.

Do not—Make the kitchen too bright—it will become an unpleasant workplace.

Do not—Have too many individual light switches—keep it simple.

DECOR

This traditional-style kitchen is a type that is readily available from many kitchen and home decoration companies. It is simple, practical, attractive, and warm. The wood-style work surfaces are economical and easy to clean. They also bring a warm tone into the room that chimes well with the duck's-egg blue of the cabinets. The blue is a homey color that creates a relaxing, friendly air. It is perfect for a family kitchen or one that friends share together. The color also enhances the sharing and social aspects of relationships.

SIMPLICITY

The key to this room is simplicity. It is not giving out any complicated messages about how sophisticated the inhabitants are, or how seriously they take cooking. It is simple, warm, and welcoming, and ready to be used. The simplicity also suits the fact that there is no eating space here. This means the space is purely functional and not a place where people are going to hang around for long periods of time. A separate dining room or eating space will compliment this practical kitchen perfectly.

ENTRANCE HALL
LIVING ROOM
KITCHEN
BEDROOM
BATHROOM

DISCUSSION
FOCUS
INSPIRATION
INTERACTION

assess, discuss, and agree

EVEN IF YOU DON'T COOK, THE STATE OF YOUR KITCHEN AND THE WAY YOU USE IT WILL HAVE AN IMPACT ON YOUR RELATIONSHIPS AND THE EMOTIONAL HEALTH OF YOUR HOME. IN ORDER TO IMPROVE THE ORGANIZATION AND AMENITIES YOUR KITCHEN PROVIDES, YOU HAVE TO CONSIDER HOW YOU USE THIS SPACE AND WHAT WOULD MAKE YOUR TIME THERE MORE ENJOYABLE.

step one

The following questionnaire will help to pinpoint how much you use the kitchen. Compare your answers with those of your partner or homesharers, and you will quickly see who uses the kitchen most, when, and for what purpose.

resolving kitchen conflict

Compare your answers with regard to who uses the kitchen, for what activity, and when this room is the busiest or least used. This exercise helps you discover just how much or how little time you spend in the kitchen. It is a good idea to discuss who does the shopping, cooking, and clearing, and whether you are happy with this arrangement.

Conflict in the kitchen can arise when too many people try to do different things at the same time. You need to agree whether your kitchen is well-designed and organized enough to provide a place for all the functions you require from it.

tick which use is appropriate to you:	PERSON A	PERSON B	PERSON C
I use the kitchen most for cooking for myself			
I use the kitchen for cooking for my:			
partner			
family			
myself			
my homemates			
I use the kitchen for getting snacks for myself			
I use the kitchen for eating:			
breakfast			
lunch			
dinner			
snacks			
I use the kitchen for			
work			
study			
play			

step two

The following questions will help you focus on how you feel about the kitchen and identify specific aspects of the kitchen that could be improved.

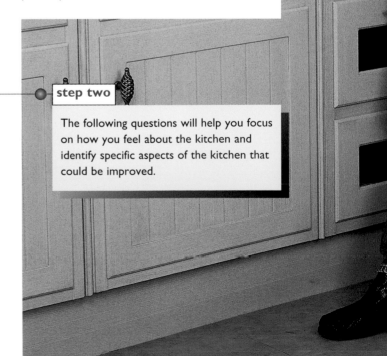

tick which use is appropriate to you:	PERSON A	PERSON B	PERSON C
I think the kitchen is messy and dirty.			
I think the kitchen needs better storage areas.			
I think the kitchen could be better organized.			
I think the cabinets need improving.			
I think the colors and decor needs updating.			
I would like better lighting in the kitchen.			
I would like to change or improve the			
preparation area			
cooking area			
sink area			
refrigerator			
I would like to entertain more in the kitchen.			
I think the kitchen needs a complete makeover.			

ask yourself:	PERSON A	PERSON B	PERSON C
What do I dislike about my main eating area?			
What priority do I give to eating?			
high			
medium			
low			
How much entertaining do I do, and would I like to entertain more?			
Discuss and agree ways of improving your eating room.			
We need to improve the colors and lighting (see focus pages 84–8).			
We need to change the table/chairs (see focus pages 86–8).			
We need to improve the furniture layout.			
We need to clear the dining table of clutter.			

kitchen sharing

First discuss the points on which you agree and what improvements you could make, and how these will alter your view and use of the kitchen.

Then discuss your differences, bearing in mind each of you will have a different view of the kitchen, depending on the tasks or activities they do there. Perhaps you should share the kitchen tasks in a different way. Come to an agreement about the improvements you should make in order to make your kitchen more functional and attractive.

a place for everything

Once you have identified how much space you actually need for each category, you have to find the best place to keep them. This will depend on the size and layout of your kitchen. For example, your cleaning, laundry, and pet products could be allocated a storage area in a utility room or under the sink while your non-perishable foods may be kept in a slide-out pantry. In a small kitchen, you could keep fresh food in wicker baskets, which keep food cool and so help your vegetables to last longer.

Once you have decided where to store the items on your list, you should put the items in each category into two piles: things that you use often and things you use occasionally. Obviously, the things that you use frequently should be in the most easily accessible areas of the kitchen.

SEE ALSO

FINDING YOUR STYLE   PAGE 18 ──○

YOUR CHANGING NEEDS   PAGE 24 ──○

SHARING A HOME   PAGE 28 ──○

PLANNING AND ORGANIZATION PAGE 142 ──○

CHAPTER

4

the bedroom

THE BEDROOM IS THE INNER SANCTUARY OF THE HOME. IN IT, YOU THROW OFF THE TRAPPINGS OF EVERYDAY LIFE AND RELAX IN COMPLETE PRIVACY. BEDROOMS CONVEY FEMININE AND NURTURING ENERGY AND IN THEM YOU CAN SURROUND YOURSELF WITH THE THINGS THAT BRING YOU PERSONAL PLEASURE. AS MULTIPURPOSE ROOMS, BEDROOMS ALSO NEED TO BE FUNCTIONAL. IF YOUR BEDROOM IS WELL PLANNED AND CONVEYS A SENSE OF TRANQUILITY, IT CAN OFFER YOU A SPECIAL COMFORT ZONE WHERE YOU CAN NURTURE YOURSELF AND SHARE INTIMATE TIMES WITH YOUR PARTNER.

bedrooms and relationships

THE BEDROOM IS NOT ONLY THE PLACE WHERE WE RENEW OUR ENERGY THROUGH SLEEP, IT IS ALSO A PLACE OF CARING, SHARING, AND INTIMACY. YOUR BEDROOM SHOULD BE A PLACE WHERE YOU ARE HAPPY TO SPEND TIME ALONE, RESTORING YOUR INNER CALM AND STRENGTH, BUT IT SHOULD ALSO BE A RELAXING OASIS WHERE YOU CAN BE INTIMATE WITH YOUR PARTNER.

So often, we devote all our attention to the activity centers in our home and neglect the more private areas like bedrooms and bathrooms. You start and end your day in the bedroom, so its impact on your life and relationships is profound. During the day we are so busy with the external demands of life that we have little time for ourselves. We need to redress the imbalance and pay more attention to creating calming places where we can relax and unwind, places where we can nurture ourselves and our relationships. The bedroom is the most important of these.

sleep center

We spend more than a third of our lives asleep. The bedroom's most important function is to provide us with a quiet and comfortable place to rest. Good sleep is one of the basic foundations of health and happiness. Getting a good night's sleep is one of the best things you can do for your health, energy level and looks. When you look and feel your best, your self-esteem will be high and your relationships can thrive.

It is essential, therefore, that a bedroom is quiet. It should be in a place that is away from any busy roads and any noisy areas of your home, such as the living room or kitchen. If this is not possible, you'll need thick interlined drapes on your windows and thick carpeting on the floor to deaden sound.

an intimate space

You'll probably spend more time with your partner in the bedroom than anywhere else so your time here must be enjoyable. Fortunately, the strongest energy in the bedroom is fire, which stokes passion and regeneration. It's not unusual for partners to turn in at different times, but going to bed at the same time is the best thing you can do to pep up your love life.

It is in your bedroom that you can really get to know one another in an intimate way. In the day, we are able to control the way people see us, but in our private spaces it is difficult to keep up a false image. When you sleep, wake up, and dress in the same room you soon get to see each other's good and bad points. Not only do you learn about each other's personal habits, you also find a way to work out a routine that allows you to use the

ENHANCING FIRE ENERGY	
1	Having varied textures in the bedroom stimulates the senses.
2	Soft lighting next to the bed creates a feeling of privacy.
3	Placing the bed so that it faces the door helps you to relax.
4	Lilac, pink, and silver colors stimulate femininity and vivid dreams.
5	Scented candles can increase sexual excitement.
6	A personal diary next to your bed helps you to indulge your fantasies.

space without conflict. An uncluttered and well laid out bedroom will ensure the space works well for dressing and grooming so that you both come out feeling and looking good.

The style in which you choose to decorate the bedroom is a very personal choice because this is a private space. Some people

WHAT YOUR BEDROOM REFLECTS ABOUT YOUR RELATIONSHIP

messy bedroom with unmade bed:	lack of self-respect and personal responsibility
a comfortable space full of personal items:	a desire for love and understanding
minimal and uncluttered room:	an intense or focused relationship
clothes strewn around the room:	irresponsibility in a relationship
a bedroom with a computer, desk:	your life is more centered on your personal skills and development than a relationship
a room with lots of sports equipment or posters of cars/planes/trains:	lots of masculine energy shows emotional immaturity and a need to prove yourself
a room full of frills, lace, soft toys:	reflects a need for romance and love over sex
a room with a big bed, or decorated in reds or silk sheets:	a relationship where sex is important
a TV in the bedroom:	reluctance to have an intimate relationship

favor a simple but practical approach that is calming and classic. For others, decorating the bedroom gives them an opportunity to indulge in a fantasy so that they can create a unique personal world. Whatever style you choose, it is important that this room gives you a sense of comfort and pleasure. By making your bedroom a special sanctuary, you will be enabling yourself to relax and let your defenses down in a secure and loving environment. In this protected space you can renew and strengthen your relationship—you will be able to love, laugh, cry, and enjoy more intimate moments together.

The bedroom is where you will share your most intimate moments with your partner, so it has a crucial role to play in the health of your relationship.

bedroom furniture and layout

IT IS VITAL THAT YOUR BEDROOM SHOULD BE COMFORTABLE AND CONVEY A FEELING OF SPACIOUSNESS, EVEN IF THE ROOM IS SMALL. THIS WILL HELP YOU TO FEEL RELAXED AND SPACIOUS ABOUT THE RELATIONSHIPS IN YOUR LIFE. THE TWO BASIC RULES FOR BEDROOMS ARE TO HAVE AS LITTLE FURNITURE AS POSSIBLE AND THEN TO PLACE WHAT YOU DO HAVE CAREFULLY.

center of attention

The bed can be as simple or as sumptuous as you desire, but it should always be the central feature in the bedroom. Other furniture should be kept to a minimum; you want to be able to walk around the bed without colliding into anything or being obstructed.

In feng shui, the life-giving force known as chi must circulate around a room with little or no interference. When chi flows smoothly and is not obstructed by large pieces of furniture or clutter, it is believed that the occupants of the room will enjoy good health and harmony in their life and relationships.

Since ancient times, we have preferred to sleep in enclosed spaces and especially in raised places, which make us feel safe and protected. A symptom of this genetic inheritance is that most people will sleep better in upstairs rooms and in beds that face the door. Feng shui consultants recommend that the bed be placed diagonally or in a position

Perhaps more than any other room, bedrooms need to be kept clear of clutter. In feng shui, an uncluttered room is said to allow healthy chi energy to circulate the room – benefiting life and relationships.

MIRROR
A full-length mirror is useful near the dressing area. It also reflects more natural light from the window around the room.

BED
The bed is placed so the door is visible from it, but not directly opposite. A trunk at the foot of the bed provides storage for blankets.

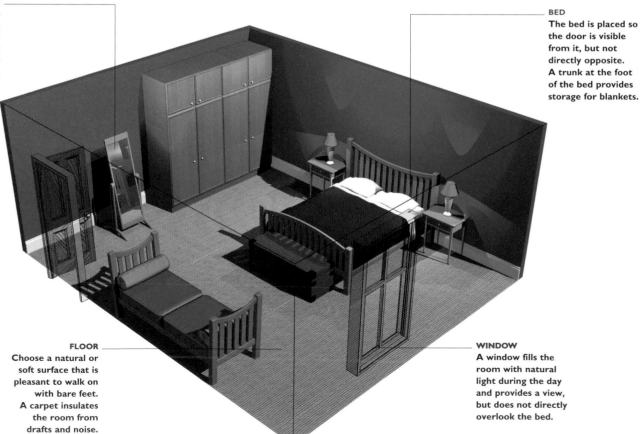

FLOOR
Choose a natural or soft surface that is pleasant to walk on with bare feet. A carpet insulates the room from drafts and noise.

WINDOW
A window fills the room with natural light during the day and provides a view, but does not directly overlook the bed.

from which there is a good view of the door so you can see anyone who enters. You should not, however, place the bed directly opposite an open door, nor directly behind it.

The natural tendency to bring items back to the nest often results in clutter accumulating around the bed. Providing a good bedside cabinet, table, or shelves solves this problem, and you can create more space by having your bedside lights on the wall rather than placed on a cabinet beside you.

plenty of storage

After the bed, the closet is the most important item in the bedroom. One of the great secrets of a calm and harmonious life is having good storage for your clothes. This allows you to get dressed and go out in a seamless, smooth operation without experiencing stress. There is nothing more irritating than not being able to find an item of clothing quickly and easily.

You need to decide whether you want freestanding or built in storage. A well designed closet is often the ideal storage solution, particularly if the space is large enough for it to incorporate drawers, shelves, and shoe racks. Other options include a pull-down ironing board, trouser press, and even a dresser. A full-length mirror is essential. If there is plenty of space in the room, a walk-in closet can elevate getting dressed into a new and exciting experience.

Some rooms are too small for a built-in closet, and it may be better to have a freestanding armoire instead. Freestanding storage makes good room dividers and can be used to partition a bedroom into a sleeping and dressing area. They are also useful for dividing space in a room that children share.

For smaller items of clothing, you'll also need a chest of drawers. Choose one to complement your bed and decorating style — a chest of drawers that has pleasing proportions and is made from quality materials can be a beautiful object in its own right.

It is also worth investing in a shoe rack, some boxes, or wicker baskets. These are invaluable for quickly storing small, troublesome items. An attractive trunk placed at the end of your bed provides a convenient place to hide extra pillows, blankets, and bedding.

If your home is large enough, you may prefer to set aside a separate room for dressing. This will leave your bedroom much clearer and with more free space. A small spare bedroom next door to the main bedroom may be a good space to convert into a walk-in closet, and there are many modern fixtures that can be installed very easily.

This attic bedroom appeals to the natural human instinct to sleep high up. The natural materials and soft lighting contribute to the cozy atmosphere, making this a good room for sleeping.

retreat space

Your bedroom not only offers you a relaxing place at night. In it you can find rest and tranquility away from the family during the day. Try to create a definite relaxation area, perhaps in a corner of the room or near a window. If there is enough space, a chaise longue is perfect for daytime relaxation in a traditional-style room. Alternatively, you can place a comfortable chair and footstool in a corner of the room where you could read or enjoy your breakfast or a cup of coffee.

bedroom colors

THE COLORS IN YOUR BEDROOM WILL REFLECT THE WAY YOU VIEW YOUR PRIVATE LIFE AND YOUR ATTITUDE TO ROMANCE. COLOR CAN BE PARTICULARLY EFFECTIVE IN CREATING A LOVING ATMOSPHERE, AND WILL THEREFORE HAVE A BIG IMPACT ON YOUR RELATIONSHIP WITH YOUR PARTNER. COLOR ALSO AFFECTS OUR ABILITY TO RELAX AND BE AT PEACE IN A PARTICULAR SPACE. IT IS CRUCIAL THAT YOU GET THE RIGHT COLOR IN THE BEDROOM TO ENHANCE ITS REGENERATIVE AND NURTURING POWERS.

To enjoy a sound sleep, you need an airy room. You are much more likely to have nightmares if your body gets too hot in the night, so it is a good idea to keep the main colors in the bedroom light and cool. Natural fabrics like silks, cottons, and linens allow the air to circulate around your bedroom and bed, so use these materials for curtains, bedding, and nightclothes.

Cool colors, such as soft green, sky blue, and lilac, have a pacifying and sedating effect on the mind and therefore help us enjoy a deep and regenerative sleep. Bright colors can be very uplifting and cheerful, and are especially useful if you find it difficult to wake up in the morning. Rich, warm colors in a bedroom are cozy and romantic, but avoid the darker colors, which can become depressing after a while.

THE COLORS OF SEX

	blood red	passion
	burgundy/wine	sensuality and loving touch
	deep rose pink	compassion and romance
	sugar pink	sentimental love and satisfying your emotional needs
	magenta	a desire to please, sacrificial or selfless love
	shocking pink	love aroused by fantasy, high expectations
	lilac/lavender	gentle, caring, and sharing attitude to love

purple haze

Purple has been used throughout history to create sacred and protected spaces for sleeping and dreaming. Violet is made from a mixture of soothing blue and stimulating red, so while this color aids rest, it is also inspiring and uplifting. While it may be unwise to decorate the bedroom entirely in purple (this will be overpowering), many find pastel tints of lilac and lavender particularly appealing.

Pale blue creates an airy atmosphere that will help to guarantee healthy sleep. It also reflects natural light, keeping the room light and positive. On the lighter end of the purple scale, this sugar-pink color will create a sensual realm for love and sleep.

SEE ALSO
COLOR PAGE 100
COMPROMISE PAGE 42
HARMONY PAGE 25
LISTENING PAGE 87

a neutral space

Neutral colors always work well in the bedroom, but avoid brilliant white, which can be stark and cold. Choose instead a soft creamy white that is softer on the eye and more flattering to the complexion. If you have a neutral color scheme, you can introduce interesting textures to provide contrast and make the room appear more comfortable and friendly.

Splashes of color on the bed, on fabric furnishings, or on small areas of the walls will bring the positive aspect of colors into the room without being overwhelming. When you want to change the mood, add a colorful throw, some cushions, or scented candles. You can change the colors according to the seasons, or put them away during the day if your bedroom is a multifunction room.

Pale pink combines the reflective and airy qualities of white with the sensual and passionate qualities of the purple range. The result is a bedroom that is both light and warm. The color also serves to maximize the sense of space in the room.

Darker colors create a cozy atmosphere, but could become overpowering. This tone of red can be used to make a large room feel snug, while a rich blue tone creates an air of calm and reflection, great for people who tend to sleep lightly.

COLOR MOODS FOR THE BEDROOM

color	mood created	best suited for use in
pale blue, green, aqua	soothing and relaxing to the mind	walls, curtains, textiles, carpet
deep, rose, or shell pink	emotionally soothing and nurturing	walls, curtains, textiles, carpet
red	sensual and sexual	cushions, bedding, nightclothes, candles, flowers
yellow	bright and cheerful	curtains, textiles
peach or apricot	warm and intimate	walls, bedding, curtains
warm beige, tan	quiet and serene	walls, carpets, bedding, furnishings
purple	luxurious and dramatic	cushions, curtains, throw
orange	cool and calm	textiles, candles, lamps
white	neutral	walls, curtains, bedding, furnishings

the sensual bedroom

THE STATE OF THE BEDROOM SAYS A LOT ABOUT YOUR ATTITUDE TO LOVE AND SEX. AN UNMADE BED AND CLOTHING STREWN ABOUT CAN REVEAL A NIGHT OF PASSION, BUT PERMANENT MESS REVEALS A LACK OF MUTUAL RESPECT. A VERY MINIMAL BEDROOM CAN REFLECT PARTNERS WHO FIND IT HARD TO EXPRESS THEIR FEELINGS.

By making your bedroom more sensual and alluring, you will feel more relaxed and sensitive to your partner's needs. To do this successfully, you need to plan your bedroom well and create balance between function and comfort. Extremes of mess and minimalism will create a hostile environment.

minimal style, minimal loving?

A streamlined and uncluttered space works well for everyday living, but may detract from more loving pastimes. So if your bedroom has a purely functional air of practicality, it will not stimulate the senses or encourage you to spend time there. Bright lights keep you focused on everyday tasks, while soft lighting and warm tones slow you down so you feel more in touch with your feelings.

A bedroom should provide a secure environment so you can relax your guard and get in touch with your emotional and physical needs. Texture is an important element for helping you drop your inhibitions. This is particularly true if your room is an uncluttered modern design. Different textures change our perception of a room so we become more conscious of the atmosphere rather than the look. When we undress, we are put directly in touch with our environment, and our senses become more alert.

Aroma is the most natural of all aphrodisiacs because it sends particular messages to the brain, thus altering our perceptions and mood. Scent plays a fundamental role in our physical make-up and can alter our behavior, so it plays an important role when it comes to attracting a mate.

Although most people use perfume to enhance their attractiveness, very few people put this knowledge to good use in their home. Taking a warm aromatic bath leaves the skin soft and scented, and if you also burn an aromatic candle, you will create an alluring atmosphere that will be hard to resist.

bedroom pampering

Healthy relationships depend on our ability to love and care for ourselves, and your bedroom is somewhere you should spend time pampering yourself. Propped up with cush-

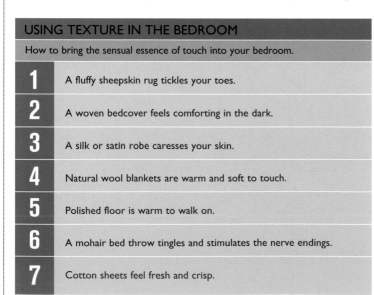

USING TEXTURE IN THE BEDROOM	
How to bring the sensual essence of touch into your bedroom.	
1	A fluffy sheepskin rug tickles your toes.
2	A woven bedcover feels comforting in the dark.
3	A silk or satin robe caresses your skin.
4	Natural wool blankets are warm and soft to touch.
5	Polished floor is warm to walk on.
6	A mohair bed throw tingles and stimulates the nerve endings.
7	Cotton sheets feel fresh and crisp.

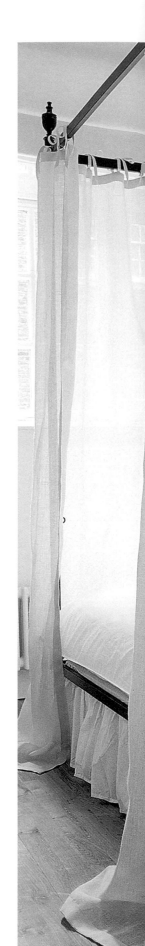

ions on your bed or in a low, comfortable chair, you can write a letter, read a book or magazine, or treat yourself to a manicure or pedicure. Spending time with yourself in a nurturing, tranquil bedroom can build up your self-esteem as well as your ability to understand and to balance your personal needs with that of your partner.

sensual lighting

To enable you to create a more romantic atmosphere in the bedroom, include some decorative lamps. Tinted bulbs give a soft glow, or you could obtain a stained glass Tiffany lamp or shade decorated with shiny glass beads to create a magical ambience. For a sensual evening together, drape your bedside light with a red, pink, or violet silk cloth (be careful not to cover the bulb) or light some aromatic candles. A floor lamp with an attractive shade makes a useful addition to light up a corner of the room to create a relaxation area away from the bed.

Allow your senses to tune into the rhythms of nature. In the morning, the sun rises, and daylight triggers changes in our metabolism to wake us up. Because our body clock is naturally in tune with daily rhythms, the ideal bedroom will face east so morning sunlight can flood the bedroom and help us to wake up feeling energetic and ready for the day ahead. If your bedroom faces another direction, hang lightweight curtains that will help the morning light to suffuse the room, while still providing privacy.

Similarly, if you have difficulty waking up and getting going in the morning, leave your curtains open a little at night to increase the amount of morning light you get. After a few days, you should find that your body becomes attuned to the natural rhythm of the day. Waking up feeling good about yourself and the world does wonders for relationships. When you are awake and alert, you are more likely to have a positive attitude to life. This natural enthusiasm is an attractive quality and will not go unnoticed by your partner.

A four-poster bed with voile draped over the posts has an airy and romantic atmosphere. The sense of light and space is enhanced by the cool tone of white chosen, creating an ethereal atmosphere.

TOP TIPS FOR A SENSUAL BEDROOM	
1	Hide everyday clutter, such as clothing, shoes, and sports equipment.
2	Turn off bright lights and close light-filtering drapes or blinds.
3	Choose bedding and linen in sensuous colors of rose pink, purple, lilac, and red.
4	Make your bed more inviting with a satin or silk throw.
5	Create a relaxing den with lots of textured scatter cushions.
6	Hang a drape over or around your bed to create a secret, intimate space.
7	Use candlelight for a soft romantic glow.
8	Soft robes and deep-pile rugs next to the bed are warm and sensual to the touch.
9	Have a tray set with a bottle of champagne or red wine and two long-stemmed cut glasses.

SEE ALSO ◆

THE HEALTHY HOME PAGE 14 —◆

CHOOSING COLOR PAGE 22 —◆

MOVING IN TOGETHER PAGE 26 —◆

LIGHT AND COLOR PAGE 150 —◆

the bed

THE BED IS ONE OF THE MOST IMPORTANT PIECES OF FURNITURE IN YOUR HOUSE AND BEARS WITNESS TO THE MOST INTIMATE MOMENTS WE SHARE. IT IS ALSO THE FIRST THING YOU NOTICE WHEN YOU ENTER A BEDROOM AND WILL SET THE TONE FOR YOUR WHOLE EXPERIENCE IN YOUR PRIVATE ROOM. YOU SHOULD BE ABLE TO TAKE PLEASURE IN LOOKING AT IT AS WELL AS LYING ON IT. IN AND AROUND YOUR BED YOU CAN CREATE A WORLD OF YOUR DREAMS THAT IS SPECIAL TO YOU AND YOUR PARTNER.

Some types of bed help to give us a feeling of enclosure and protection: old-fashioned beds are extremely high off the ground for this reason, and sleeping platforms can be intriguing whatever your age. You can also easily create a feeling of privacy and protection by choosing a four-poster bed or by draping your bed with a canopy. Soft, flowing fabrics create a dreamy, exotic feeling that is most enticing, and thicker fabrics can create a secret space inside. Draped beds are making a comeback, and provide a wonderful central focus in a small room. They can also enrich an uncluttered minimal bedroom.

headboards

A headboard is not only practical, it is the crowning glory of the bed. Remember that the headboard is likely to get dirty, so darker colors and washable fabrics work best. If you want to honor your partnership in a spiritual way, hang a religious symbol such as an angel, above the bed to bless and protect you while you sleep.

CHOOSING A BED
Think about the type of relationship you enjoy—or want to enjoy—before buying your bed.

FOUR-POSTER
In this romantic bed, you can create your own little world, protected and hidden from the rest of the house. It provides an intimate and sacred space that helps you to feel a special connection with someone you love. Four-posters needn't be old-fashioned; there are many modern designs made from wood, bamboo, and metal.

FUTON
This traditional Japanese mattress is easy to roll up and move around. Some modern versions have wooden slatted bases that can be turned into seats during the day. Futons have a natural, unpretentious look and suit a couple who enjoy simplicity. Sleeping low to the floor promotes a feeling of security and honesty.

ORIENTAL
Oriental-style beds can give an exotic and mysterious feel to a bedroom. Many oriental beds are made from rattan or carved wood, or a combination. The textures, rich colors, and natural scent of the materials can help you feel pampered and special.

crucial comfort

Make a strong statement in your bedroom and choose as large a bed as you can. Most double beds range from 4 feet 6 inches (1.37m) to 6 feet (1.83m) in width, actually allowing each person less space to sleep than they enjoyed as a child.

When selecting a mattress, you need to lie on it with your partner. If the mattress is too firm and unyielding, you will feel pressure on your hips, and you will end up tossing and turning to try to find a comfortable position. If the mattress is too soft, you will both roll into the middle and wake up with backache. If your partner likes a different firmness from you, find a mattress that is different on each side. You could also incorporate two mattresses into a single bed frame or buy a dual mattress that allows you to change your sleeping position independently.

pillow talk

Choosing the right pillow is essential if you are to enjoy a good night's sleep. Curled feather pillows are warm, light, and airy, but some people are allergic to the feathers and prefer a polyester and cotton pillow.

dress it up

There is nothing more enticing than a well-made bed. A beautiful bedcover or quality sheets will soothe you after a hard day.

White and cream remain the most popular colors for bed linen. Natural materials like cotton allow your skin to breathe and air to flow around the bed. Neutral colors look good with any style bedroom and last longer as the colors won't fade or run. Sheets and pillowcases in small checks or stripes also look fresh and attractive. Personalize plain bed linen with the addition of a sumptuous silk or satin bedcover to create an air of luxury.

TRADITIONAL METAL BED

A traditional bedstead creates an old-fashioned country look, which is perfect for a couple who have traditional values and a romantic view of relationships. However, metal bars can have a subtly restraining feel.

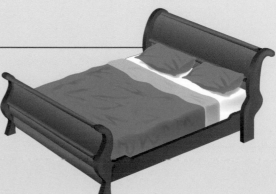

SLEEK MODERN

Most modern beds are low and have clean uncluttered lines, which give them a feeling of openness. When you lie on this type of bed you feel free of constraint, making them perfect for a relaxed informal lifestyle. Some have an integral headboard and side tables, that move around on hinges. Other beds incorporate movable mattresses, allowing flexibility of sleeping positions.

SLEIGH BED

A Lit Bateaux bed has a timeless elegance, and its sensuous curves reflect a couple who are able to express their emotions and physical needs. The sleigh shape can help to evoke the feeling that you are on your own special journey to a magical place.

de-clutter your bedroom

THE RELATIONSHIP YOU HAVE WITH YOUR BEDROOM IS DIRECTLY CONNECTED TO THE WAY YOU VIEW AND CARE FOR YOURSELF. IF YOU ALLOW YOUR BEDROOM TO BECOME CLUTTERED AND MESSY, IT NOT ONLY REFLECTS A LACK OF RESPONSIBILITY, BUT CAN UNDERMINE YOUR CAPACITY FOR SELF-LOVE. TAKING CARE OF YOUR BEDROOM WILL HELP YOU TO NURTURE SELF-ESTEEM AND BUILD A GOOD SELF-IMAGE THAT WILL IN TURN ENHANCE YOUR ABILITY TO MAINTAIN STRONG, LOVING RELATIONSHIPS.

Regularly cleaning your bedroom and keeping it clear is more important than in other areas. A messy bedroom can lower your respect for your partner. If you are single, it will reflect negatively on your ability to establish and maintain a good relationship.

clothing clutter

A common cause of conflict in a relationship is dirty clothing left on the floor. Someone who is in the habit of leaving clothing around the bedroom is often a person who is always in a hurry or preoccupied with other things, neither of which help a loving relationship.

By clearing up after your partner you are taking on the role of a parent, inappropriate in an equal partnership. Leaving clothing lying around is usually due to a lack of awareness. Once you have drawn your partner's attention to it and explained that a messy bedroom makes you feel angry and hurt, a caring partner will improve his or her ways.

behind closed doors

Many bedrooms appear clean and neat on the surface, but behind the closet doors and in the drawers the real mess lurks unseen. Superficial neatness such as this may fool

The stark contrast between a black bed frame and pillows with the white walls and bed linen help to create an air of cleanliness and order. The sculptural posts of the bed add a touch of variety to stop the room from looking too much like a cell.

CLEAR UP YOUR CLOSET

Looking into a well-organized closet can prove to be a very satisfying experience since it makes choosing clothes and coordinating an outfit much easier. To clear up your closet, create more space, and help you maintain your closet in a neat state, follow these easy steps:

1 Make specific places for items such as socks, belts, scarves, ties, jewelry.

2 Take out all your coats and bulky items and store them in a separate place.

3 If you go to work every day, keep a section of your closet devoted to work clothes and make sure you always have a clean set ready for the morning.

4 Put the clothes you wear the most in the most accessible part of the closet.

5 Place close together clothes of similar color so you can quickly mix and match.

6 Keep a special area on one side for evening wear and special clothes.

7 Get a drawer divider that allows you to sort out socks and underclothes.

8 Store your shoes in boxes and stick a Polaroid of the shoes on the outside of the box.

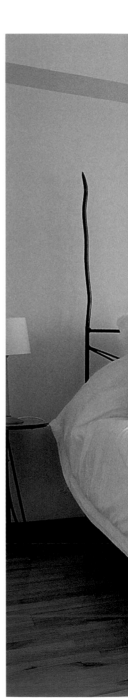

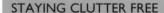

other people entering your bedroom, but it won't fool you. Knowing you have hidden clutter waiting to be dealt with can be like trying to keep a guilty secret. It eats away from the inside, causing you stress. In many ways, this can be more destructive than visible mess since it implies dishonesty and can cause you to feel uneasy with yourself.

Most people have too many clothes. We are often happy to get rid of other items around the home once they become outdated, but we hang onto old clothing. Many people keep outfits and even shoes that they have long outgrown in the hope that they will slim down enough to wear them again. Or they keep them for sentimental reasons.

Do yourself—and whoever you share your bedroom with—a favor and clear your old clothes out of your closet. Throw or give away any items that you have not worn for more than two years. When you have done this, you will be left with a selection of clothing that more accurately reflects your true self and your present lifestyle.

STAYING CLUTTER FREE

If your bedroom is to stay clean and neat, you have to work at it. Little chores done every day keep your bedroom clean and inviting, so work out a routine together and stick to it.

EVERY DAY

Make your bed.
Hang up your clothes when you go to bed or before you leave the room.
Take any cups or glasses into the kitchen.
Put any unnecessary papers into a box for recycling.

WEEKLY

Open the windows and air the room.
Air your bedclothes by leaving your bed unmade for an hour or two.
Vacuum the floor.
Clean your bedside table.
Do the laundry.
Put flowers next to your bed.
Water your plants.

MONTHLY

Clean your windows inside and out.
Give the room a good airing.
Clean your bedside table, drawers, or cupboards.
Clean and polish your shoes.

SEASONAL

Pack away items of your wardrobe you do not need for the season.
Sort out items you do not wear.
Turn your mattress.
Change your bed linen and perhaps even bedroom decor to suit the season.

SEE ALSO

MINIMALIST OR COZY LIVING? PAGE 20

THE ART OF FENG SHUI PAGE 148

LIGHT AND COLOR PAGE 150

rhapsody in white

WHITE IS NOT ALWAYS COLD. DEPENDING ON THE COLORS AND TEXTURES THAT ACCOMPANY IT, WHITE CAN LOOK AIRY AND ROMANTIC. THIS BEDROOM MAKES THE MOST OF WHITE'S FRESHNESS BY CONTRASTING IT WITH WARM WOOD COLORS.

COMPOSITION

This subtly decorated room makes the most of light, white fabric to create a magical space within a simple bedroom. Above the bed, the fabric is gathered to a central point, forming a cascade down and around the headboard. This can serve as a mosquito net in warm climates or simply to create a private space around the bed. The curtains echo the same effect, allowing light to pour in through the window.

UPLIFTING

The effect of all this floaty material is to draw the eye up. This can actually cause you to feel elated, and makes the room especially romantic. No one entering this room could stop their heart from beating a little faster at the messages of love and inspiration that it seems to communicate. A room like this demonstrates the importance of love in your life, while retaining a certain sense of mystery.

COLORS

Bright white on its own can be uncompromising and cold. To make sure this room keeps its romantic air without being too white and cold, a few subtle touches have been made. The first is to make a contrast with the white with the warm wood colors of the bed, bedside chest, and the flooring. These are all in harmony with each other, so the overall cohesion of the room is not threatened. A touch of green from the flower in the corner also contributes a vital rest for the eye.

PAINT EFFECT

The paint on the wall is not applied in a solid coat. It has been applied so areas of the color underneath show through. This mottled effect breaks up the monotony of the wall, which could be overpowering if it was utterly white. The undercolor also echoes with the warm wood tones in the room. It also helps to enhance the effect of the draped material, adding to the impression of suffused light. The whole effect is like looking into a heavenly cloud.

TEXTURE

Texture is as important as color in this room. The simplicity of the colors and the limited tonal range focus the attention onto the textures within the room. For this reason the reassuring presence of the solid wood objects is vitally important to the theme. In the midst of all the airy, cloudlike whiteness, you need something solid on which to rest your eye and your touch. The wood provides this. It is a wonderful combination: the room keeps your feet grounded, while offering your head a heavenly aspect. The wood will therefore help the relationships taking place here to remain grounded and real.

LIGHTING

This lighting of the room is as effective at night as during the day. We can see how the natural light suffuses the room through the thin, white fabric. At night, the warmer light of a bedside lamp creates an intimate space within the larger expanse of the room. This warm light will reflect off the various white surfaces, providing a wonderfully romantic setting. The candle is a perfect romantic symbol, but should not be lit for safety reasons.

fantasy room

YOUR BEDROOM IS YOUR VERY OWN PLACE OF DREAMS. GOVERNED BY THE FIRE ELEMENT, IT IS A PLACE OF INSPIRATION AND PASSION. WHY BE RESTRAINED WHEN YOU CAN CREATE A SPECIAL REALM WITHIN YOUR BEDROOM'S FOUR WALLS?

MAGIC CARPET

It is surprisingly easy and economical to change your bedroom into an exotic realm. With a few well-chosen colors and materials, you can take yourself on a trip to any destination in the world. Your imagination is the only limit. And this isn't about childish fantasy or mindless escapism. Using your imagination in this way can help you to open new aspects within yourself and within your relationship.

CHOOSE YOUR DESTINATION

If you share a bedroom with your partner, the whole exercise of creating an exotic room can enhance your sense of fun and togetherness. Make sure it is a joint project and not dominated by one or other partner. You could choose a style that reflects a place you both have happy memories of, or you could go for somewhere neither of you has been.

LIGHT YOUR FIRES

Sleeping in a room like this will encourage you to be more spontaneous and creative. This new impetus will affect your relationships as well as your life in general. It is a perfect exercise for a couple who are having trouble bringing enough spark and life into their relationship. The key stage to get through is your natural feelings of inhibition and reserve. Even if the room looks silly to other people, it is a project that you have worked on together and will bring you closer together.

COLOR THERAPY

A key part of a fantasy room's beneficial effect on your relationship is that it will bring new, vibrant colors into your life. Instead of the usual subdued colors that we use for the rest of the home, you can really explore some of the more exotic reaches of the palette. Luxurious effects and valuable-looking materials all stress the fact that you value your relationship and are willing to put time and effort into it. So the more colorful, the better.

PERSIAN PALACE

In this case, the couple have gone for a North African or Middle Eastern idyll. Rich tones of blue create an atmosphere that is all about right here, right now. It literally creates a sky around the room, making this room a world of its own. Blue is a deeply relaxing color, while turquoise helps communication and understanding. The blue is contrasted by the vibrant reds, yellows, and oranges of the bedcover, adding the all-important spark of passion.

INSPIRATION

All of the colors used here are typical of Muslim countries such as Iraq and Iran, the center of the ancient kingdom of Persia. To western minds, the word Persia brings the suggestion of splendid luxury, spices, and ornate palaces and mosques in turquoise and blue. This region and period in history is a rich source of inspiration for interior designers all over the world and is especially suitable for a relaxing, intimate space.

MAKING SPACE

The draped swathes of turquoise fabric form a canopy over the bed. This type of enclosed space can make the bed a much more intimate and cozy space. This helps you focus on your relationship rather than what is going on in other areas of your life. We all need these special places that are set aside for particular purposes. They act as the energy centers for important emotional centers of our lives and demonstrate the priority that we give them. Important areas such as relationships, family, work, health, and the self all warrant a space of their own somewhere in your home.

SPACE MAKERS

In this case, a space has been made using draped fabric. This has the advantage of providing a color and texture, as well as marking out the space. You can use various other techniques to create special spaces within the home. The layout of your furniture and careful use of lighting or color can all be harnessed to highlight an area of a room. They don't have to be large—in some cases it might just be part of a shelf—but they serve the purpose of acknowledging the important things in your life and help you stay focused on them.

assess, discuss, and agree

THE GOAL WITHIN THE BEDROOM IS TO BALANCE YOUR OWN NEEDS WITH THOSE OF YOUR PARTNER. THIS MEANS MAKING SURE THE ROOM WORKS WELL FOR EACH OF YOU AS INDIVIDUALS AND AS A COUPLE. THINK FIRST ABOUT HOW YOU USE YOUR BEDROOM AS AN INDIVIDUAL AND THEN DISCUSS THE TIMES YOU USE IT AS A COUPLE. LOOK AT THE LAYOUT OF THE ROOM, THE BED ITSELF, STORAGE SPACE, AND ATMOSPHERE.

Use step one to discuss whether you enjoy being in your bedroom, and what activities you would like to do there. This exercise also helps you discover who does most of the bedroom chores. Discuss whether you are happy with this arrangement. Conflict in the bedroom can arise when partners have different routines, making getting up and dressing difficult.

room for two

After you have answered the questions in step two, discuss the points on which you both agree regarding the improvements you could make and how these will alter your view and use of the bedroom.

Then discuss your differences, bearing in mind that each of you will have a different view of the bedroom, depending on the tasks or activities you do there. If you spend little time together in the bedroom, you should agree on ways to make the room more enticing. Come to an agreement about improvements that will make your bedroom both more functional and more attractive.

step one

The following questionnaire will to help to pinpoint how you use your bedroom. Compare your answers with those of your partner, and you will quickly see whether your bedroom is meeting both of your needs.

check which use is appropriate to you:	PERSON A	PERSON B	PERSON C
I usually get up…			
earlier than my partner			
later than my partner			
at the same time as my partner			
I usually go to bed …			
earlier than my partner			
later than my partner			
at the same time as my partner			
I get dressed in the bedroom			
I do my personal grooming in the bedroom			
I sleep well and wake up refreshed			
I also use my bedroom for…			
work			
study			
reading			
watching TV			
entertaining			
eating			
I would like my bedroom to be more…			
relaxing			
sensual			
comfortable			
I usually…			
make the bed			
clear up			

People get territorial about their bedroom. Coming up with a plan here makes for a great bonding exercise.

step two

You need to agree whether your bedroom is comfortable, well-designed, and organized enough to provide a place for all the functions you require. This can be an interesting exercise for a couple, as it focuses on how each partner views the bedroom. Very often, each partner has very different ideas about the functions that the bedroom should perform. This is one room where compromise is the most important ingredient. A balanced bedroom should show characteristics of both partners, rather than one dominating. The following questions will help you focus on how you feel about the bedroom and identify aspects that could be improved.

tick which use is appropriate to you:	PERSON A	PERSON B	PERSON C
I think the bedroom is a messy and dirty place.			
I need better storage areas for my…			
clothing			
shoes			
jewelry			
coats			
sports clothes			
underclothes			
socks			
hats			
I think the closets need reorganizing.			
I think the bed is too…			
soft			
hard			
small			
I think the decor needs to be changed.			
I would like better…			
lights next to the bed			
side lighting			
lighting over the dressing area			
I think the bedroom needs a makeover.			

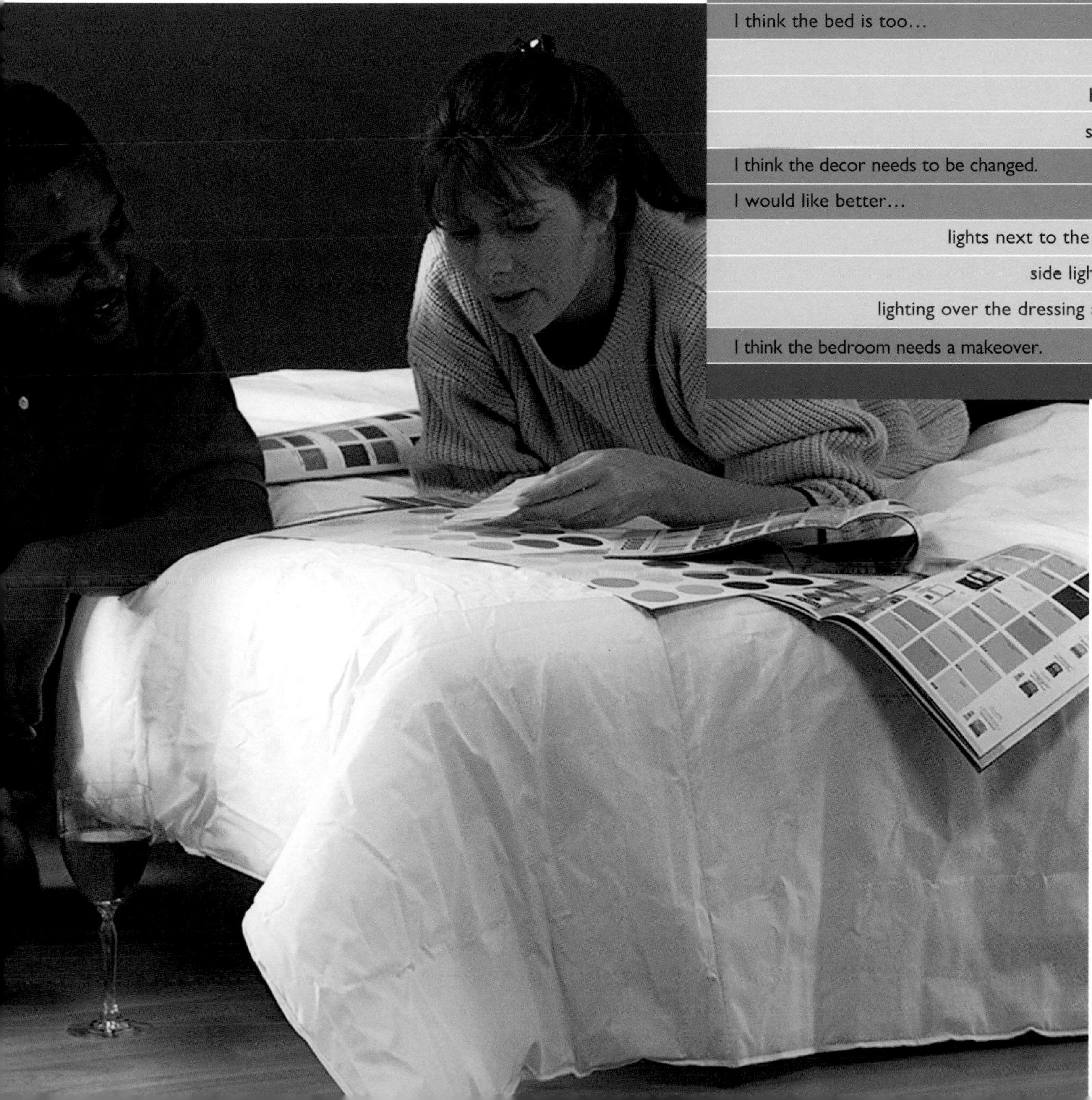

SEE ALSO

THE HEALTHY HOME PAGE 14
CHOOSING COLOR PAGE 22
MOVING IN TOGETHER PAGE 26
LIGHT AND COLOR PAGE 150

CHAPTER

5

bathrooms

IN THIS BUSY WORLD WE ALL NEED PRIVACY AND TIME TO UNWIND. YOUR BATHROOM CAN BE THE PERFECT

RETREAT WHERE YOU CAN REFRESH BOTH BODY AND SOUL. BATHING WASHES AWAY THE PHYSICAL AND

EMOTIONAL POLLUTION WE PICK UP DURING THE DAY, LEAVING US REFRESHED AND REVITALIZED. WHILE

YOU ARE TAKING A SHOWER OR BATH, THE HEALING POWER OF WATER HELPS YOU GET IN TOUCH WITH

YOUR EMOTIONS AND EMPOWERS YOU TO EXPRESS YOUR FEELINGS. BY IMPROVING YOUR BATHROOM, YOU

WILL NATURALLY IMPROVE COMMUNICATION WITHIN YOUR RELATIONSHIPS.

how the bathroom affects relationships

YOUR BATHROOM SHOULD NOT JUST BE A PLACE FOR A SPEEDY WASH AND BRUSH; IT SHOULD BE SOMEWHERE YOU ENJOY SPENDING TIME AND WHERE YOU CAN TAKE PLEASURE IN CARING FOR YOURSELF. ALTHOUGH YOUR BATHROOM SHOULD ALLOW YOU PERSONAL PRIVACY WHEN YOU NEED IT, IT MIGHT ALSO HAVE TO BE A LIVELY SPACE THAT YOU CAN SHARE WITH YOUR PARTNER AND CHILDREN.

Water has many wonderful properties that can enhance your health and well-being. There is nothing more invigorating than a taking a shower in the morning to prepare you for the day. A good shower stimulates your nerve endings, making you feel alive and alert. The negative ions produced by moving water makes showering a wonderful way to ease stress-related problems. Washing your hair and shaving are also refreshing rituals that can be enjoyable if your bathroom is attractive and well designed.

In the evening your bathroom can perform another vital function. A long soak in the bath can help you relax and forget the pressures of the day. In the bathroom we connect with the element of water, which washes away tension, especially in the shoulders, chest, and throat. Bathing is a natural way to detoxify the body and improve vitality. If you bathe before going to bed it can also help you get to sleep.

The design and atmosphere in your bathroom will have a big impact on your life. A bright and light bathroom creates a healthy

Like all rooms in the home, your bathroom should reflect your personal taste and personality. If a metal tub, a jug of warm water, and candlelight does it for you—then go with it.

HOW TO ENHANCE THE WATER ENERGY

- ■ Wavy lines and shapes are soothing to the emotions.
- ■ A power shower makes you feel more alert and alive.
- ■ Soft music in the bathroom can help you to reflect on your problems.
- ■ Listening to the sounds of the sea in a conch or cowrie shell can soothe you.
- ■ Mirrors reflect water energy and bring abundance into your life.
- ■ Looking at the sky through a window or skylight will help you to unwind.
- ■ Soft, white towels reflect the cleanliness and softness of water energy.

and relaxing environment for personal grooming. It also reflects a willingness to prioritize your need for inner replenishment and peace. How much care you take with your appearance says a lot about you as a person as well as the amount of effort you are willing to put into a relationship. Looking after your body demonstrates personal responsibility and your ability to care and value yourself as well as your partner. On the other hand, an unhealthy obsession with your looks and appearance can reflect someone who is insecure and self-centered.

the energy of water

The healing power of water can bring balance into your life and relationships. Bathing not only cleanses your body, it can enhance your moods and emotions. In nature the rise and fall of ocean tides is closely linked to the moon, which also influences the water flowing through our body. Water links our internal cycles to the natural rhythms around us, bringing our whole system into balance. Taking a bath or shower offers a reconnection with this healing and balancing substance, washing away fears, anger, and pain, and leaving you feeling emotionally cleansed.

The time you spend unwinding in the bathroom can help you assess many things about your life and relationships. The water element enhances the flow of communication, both inwardly and with other people. During a bath we have private time for self-reflection. The healing power of water helps release negative thought and behavioral patterns so we become more flexible and open-minded in our relationships. It is not unusual for the release of emotional energy in the bath or shower to be accompanied by a desire to whistle, hum, or sing. Afterwards you feel really relaxed and better able to express your thoughts and feelings. This is a good time to have a "heart to heart" with your partner.

a social space

It is only relatively recently that bathing has become a private affair. Throughout history the bath house was a social place, somewhere to relax, meet friends and even do business. Nowadays, we usually bathe alone, but a well-designed bathroom and shower can also give you the opportunity to enjoy the social aspects of bathing. Even in a standard-sized bathroom, it is often possible to replace a standard tub with a corner bath or a double shower unit. Try to make your bathroom more comfortable and relaxed by adding a stool or chair. This encourages you to spend more time there but also offers a place to sit and chat to your partner while he or she is bathing. Sharing the bathroom encourages intimacy and sharing within your relationship.

When you have more space, you can create a relaxing oasis where you can spend time together. Washing and grooming each other is a very intimate activity that can bring you together. By creating a relaxing mood in your bathroom, bathing becomes a pleasurable and sensual experience.

YOUR BATHROOM, YOUR RELATIONSHIP

THE WAY YOU USE YOUR BATHROOM CAN BRING ADDED BENEFITS TO YOUR RELATIONSHIP WITH A PARTNER. TRY THESE IDEAS:

Bring more laughter into your relationship by sharing a shower.

Set a romantic mood by taking a relaxing soak together.

Star-gaze from a hot tub or outdoor Jacuzzi.

Sing in the shower to help your powers of communication.

The aroma of an exotic bath elixir stimulates the senses.

A shower can cleanse the mind and purify the soul after a disagreement.

Add a touch of luxury by giving your partner a glass of champagne when they are in the bathtub.

Designate time after a bath for a "heart to heart."

ENTRANCE HALL
LIVING ROOM
KITCHEN
BEDROOM
BATHROOM

DISCUSSION
FOCUS
INSPIRATION
INTERACTION

bathroom design, layout, and storage

BATHROOMS NEED TO BE INCREDIBLY FLEXIBLE SO THAT THEY ARE FUNCTIONAL BUT ALSO GIVE YOU THE OPPORTUNITY TO RELAX ALONE AND WITH A PARTNER. EVEN SMALL BATHROOMS CAN BE DESIGNED TO OFFER YOU DIFFERENT BATHING OPTIONS AND A PLACE TO SIT WHILE YOUR PARTNER HAS A SOAK.

The bathroom is usually the smallest room in the house, so it requires special planning and constant maintenance. The options for a bathroom layout may be limited, so you should first decide whether you want both a shower and bathtub in the same room. Ideally, you would have more than one bathroom in your home, as well as a separate toilet. This arrangement means your main bathroom remains comfortable and private, and you can organize it to suit yourself. A second bathroom could be more utilitarian and equipped with a shower for quick washing.

The layout of most bathrooms depends entirely on where the bathtub is placed. Often there is only one suitable position, and this is largely to do with the plumbing. Today there are bathtubs of various shapes—you should be able to find one to suit any room. Large tubs require lots of water, so make sure you have an adequate hot water supply.

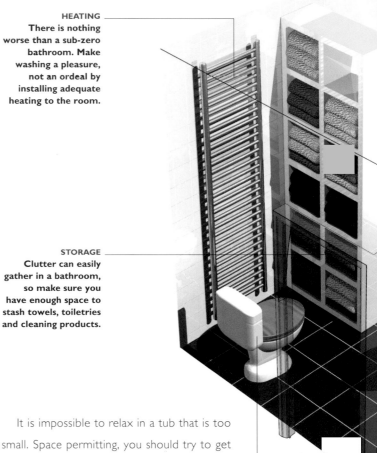

HEATING
There is nothing worse than a sub-zero bathroom. Make washing a pleasure, not an ordeal by installing adequate heating to the room.

STORAGE
Clutter can easily gather in a bathroom, so make sure you have enough space to stash towels, toiletries and cleaning products.

TOILET
The toilet should preferably be out of sight from the rest of the bathroom. Here, it is separated by a towel shelf; you could also use a screen.

CREATE A WET ROOM

Designing a bathroom from scratch can offer you the opportunity to create a wet room. This allows you great freedom to move around when taking a shower—making it fun and liberating, and great for a shared bathing experience.

For a wet room, the room should be designed so the whole floor and the walls are waterproof, and the water drains away through a central waste hole in the floor. Cover the walls and floors with colorful mosaics or tiles, or for a more modern look, use varnished chipboard or waterproof linoleum panels.

It is impossible to relax in a tub that is too small. Space permitting, you should try to get one that allows you to stretch out. Long bathtubs are ideal for a long relaxing soak on your own. A normal-sized bath is 66 inches (1700mm) in length and 27 inches (700mm) wide. This allows one adult to bathe in comfort, allowing him or her to straighten the legs in the water. Modern tubs are contoured and can provide head and arm rests. If you have an older-style tub, you can still enjoy more comfort by using a bath pillow. Most tubs give you the option of side grips to help you get in and out, and reduce the possibility of slipping.

BATHTUB
Your bathtub should be large enough to be comfortable, but not so big that it drains your hot water supply.

SKYLIGHT
A window or skylight visible from the bathtub transforms the experience of bathing into a truly relaxing and refreshing one.

SHOWER
A shower gives you the option of a quick wash and can help save time if partners need to wash at the same time.

FLOORING
Use a natural surface for the floor, such as varnished wood or stone. This will give the bathroom an earthy quality.

BASIN
A traditional basin adds a wholesome touch to the scheme.

Depending on where the door is located, a corner bathtub can free up space in a small bathroom. Corner tubs come in many shapes and sizes—some can accommodate up to three people. If you get a corner tub for two, remember to place the faucets centrally so you can both rest your head with ease.

Other considerations for bathroom layout include the placing of the basin and toilet. It is best to locate the toilet away from the door so it is hidden from view. Basins can be free-standing or built-in, but always make sure they are large enough to use without spilling water on the floor. Put a storage shelf or cupboard with essential items like toothbrushes and soap within easy reach, but do not place a high shelf directly over the basin or you will bump your head.

showers

Taking a bath is fine when you have plenty of time to relax, but for many people a shower is more enjoyable and offers much more flexibility. Whereas a bath is relaxing, a shower is bracing and invigorating. You can take a shower in the morning before work, during a hot day, or after a sports activity. Showers are economical with water and can fit into small spaces, so they are ideal for small bathrooms. If you don't have room for a shower in the bathroom, you may be able to fit one into an alcove, attic, garage, or shed.

The secret to having a really good shower is water pressure. There is nothing worse than standing under a little dribble of water. For a shower to work well, you need a powerful jet of water coming from a well-designed shower head or from jets located at different heights in the cubicle. This means all parts of your body get warm and wet. Check your

water system before installing a shower so you know whether you need an electric pump to boost the pressure.

Many homes have shower rooms that are shared by different family members and guests of all shapes and sizes. Attaching the shower head to a movable arm on an upright rod will allow the user to alter its height to make the shower enjoyable whether he or she is a child or a six-foot adult.

Shower cubicles and trays are often too small, so make sure you have enough space to move around without knocking your elbows against the walls. Showering can be messy, and leaving a bathroom floor and walls wet will not impress other bathroom users. To prevent water from splashing around the room, have a large shower cubicle with doors, or install a wider-than-normal bathtub with a good shower screen. The base of a shower is usually made from acrylic, but for a more substantial base you can create your own floor using tiles or mosaics. Also make sure you can reach your towel from inside the shower, or you will drip water on the floor.

color and lighting

THERE IS NOTHING WORSE THAN A DREARY BATHROOM. IF YOUR BATHROOM IS MESSY, DARK, AND UNATTRACTIVE, YOU WILL SPEND LITTLE TIME THERE, AND VERY SOON YOU WILL FEEL IRRITABLE AND TIRED. CHANGING THE COLORS AND LIGHTING IN YOUR BATHROOM CAN HAVE AN IMMEDIATE IMPACT ON YOUR MOOD AND COMPLETELY CHANGE YOUR ATTITUDE TO BATHING.

We all dream of having a bathroom with a view. Taking a shower out of doors or lying in a bathtub looking out into nature is a wonderfully therapeutic and uplifting experience. Sunlight helps regulate our internal body clock, which in turn energizes our whole system. So if your bathroom has a window, make the most of the natural light and air. Unfortunately, most bathrooms overlook a neighbor or a public place, so unless you are very lucky, you will need to install etched or obscured glass in the window. Other options that give you privacy but still allow light in are one-way glass, glass bricks, or stained glass panels. Venetian blinds and wooden shutters also offer flexibility, so you can see out but maintain your privacy.

Although you need good directional light over a mirror, your bathroom need not be lit up like a football field. Fluorescent strip lights in the bathroom cast a harsh and unflattering light, so they are best avoided. Looking tired and drawn in the mirror does nothing for your self-esteem and will encourage you to avoid spending time in the bathroom. Choose a halogen light, which is closer to natural sunlight. If you have warm-colored tiles and colors in the bathroom, the light reflected from them will give your skin a warm glow. People tend to feel much more comfortable and relaxed in a warm-colored bathroom, espe-

cially when sharing a bath with a partner. Make sure, too, that you don't position a ceiling light where it will shine in your eyes when you are trying to relax in the bath—it will have the opposite effect on you.

Even if there is good natural light, you will still need additional lighting for shaving, grooming, and applying makeup. Rather than using lights around a mirror, place an adjustable low-voltage downlight in the ceiling. Position it away from the wall so light bounces off the white basin. This way, your face will be lit evenly from below and above.

colors for bathrooms

When we think of water, we naturally think of white surf, blue skies, and sparkling turquoise water. These cool and refreshing colors are ideal for your bathroom, especially if you want to create a soothing and relaxing space. White is very purifying, and blue and green are both relaxing and refreshing to the mind. Cool colors are practical, too, and are useful for internal bathrooms, which may get hot and stuffy. These tones would also suit your bathroom if you live in a hot climate. Warm-colored towels and accessories will warm up a white or cool bathroom in winter.

If you live in a cold climate or have a dark bathroom, it would be much better to incorporate warm, earthy colors into the room.

A combination of white walls, white porcelain and the natural brown of a wood floor make this bathroom both airy and earthy. A sunken bath enhances the idea of immersion that makes bathing so regenerative.

BATHROOM MOODS

THINK ABOUT THE EFFECT DIFFERENT COLORS WILL HAVE ON YOU BEFORE CHOOSING ONE FOR YOUR BATHROOM.

White is cleansing to the body and purifying to the soul.

Blue is cooling and relaxing to the mind.

Green is relaxing to the mind and balances the emotions.

Turquoise is refreshing and restorative to the body and mind.

Ocher/brown is natural, relaxing, and grounding.

Cream/peach/rose is gently warming and nurturing.

Terracotta/burnt orange is warming and relaxes the emotions.

Purple is luxurious and opulent (use for accent only).

The natural warmth and beauty of wooden floors and furniture can bring a bathroom to life. Warm pink, peach, or terracotta tiles or walls create an emotionally supportive and relaxing interior that can make your bathroom more intimate and luxurious.

Paint finishes such as dragging and marbling work well in a bathroom because the glaze is waterproof and gives a lovely reflective glow in the evening. Creating a paint effect has never been easier, and manufacturers now supply kits with easy-to-follow instructions. Small bathrooms and shower rooms are better fully tiled, but remember that tiles are difficult and expensive to change. So for maximum flexibility, it is better to stick to white or neutral, and add a colored or patterned border tile. In a simple neutral bathroom, you can quickly alter the mood by introducing changes in your towels, soaps, and bath accessories.

bathroom sanctuary

EVEN IF YOU SHARE YOUR PLACE WITH A LOVING PARTNER, YOU STILL NEED TO RESPECT EACH OTHER'S PRIVACY. WE ARE NATURALLY DRAWN TO WATER WHEN WE ARE TIRED AND STRESSED OUT, AND THERE ARE FEW PEOPLE WHO DO NOT FIND THIS NATURAL ELEMENT VERY HEALING. THE BATHROOM IS THE PERFECT RETREAT WHERE YOU CAN SPEND SOME TIME REVITALIZING BOTH BODY AND SOUL.

Water therapy has been used for centuries for healing and for beauty treatments. Water has amazing properties that can enhance your health and well-being. It is also a natural way to detoxify the mind and body. By combining bathing with essential oils, mud and face packs, sea salt, or seaweed, you can turn a simple bath into a truly revitalizing cleansing ritual.

Having a bath or shower may be the only time you have to yourself during the day—so make the most of it. Pick a time when all your chores are done and you can spend some time pampering yourself without feeling guilty. Your partner may also appreciate some time alone while you are bathing; and afterward your bathed and scented body may prove irresistible to him or her.

When you are ready to take a bath, make sure you have everything you need close at hand so you don't have to get out of the tub to reach for some soap or a towel. While you are running the water, light some candles and play some soft music to set the scene.

luxury bathing

Spa baths used to be found only in health resorts and hotels, but they are growing in popularity for home bathing. Spending time relaxing in a bubbling spa bath can be a wonderfully relaxing and revitalizing experience.

Spa baths have hidden benefits and have been found not only to reduce fatigue but to boost potency and fertility. Unfortunately, they are still fairly expensive. A more economical alternative is to get spa jets installed in your standard bathtub. Choose the maximum number of jets you can so you don't end up with a pathetic few bubbles. Or simply turn an ordinary bathtub into a home spa by filling it with a luxury bubble bath elixir.

If your place has a little-used bedroom, you could turn it into a luxurious bathroom retreat. In an older-style home, you may have a fireplace in this room, while a large window with a view would be an added bonus. A freestanding bathtub is perfect for such a luxury bathroom as well as an old-fashioned basin and toilet with brass fixtures. Fill your bathroom retreat with exotic plants and indulge yourself by introducing a comfortable chair, a decorative chest of drawers, and even splurge on a Persian rug.

an outdoor spa

If you have an outdoor area that is accessible to the bedroom, or cloakroom facilities in a garage or shed, you could indulge yourselves with a hot tub. These are very economical compared to a swimming pool and can bring you enjoyment throughout the seasons. Incorporate a hot tub into your deck or patio

and screen it from view with foliage. In this natural setting the aroma of the wood and the warm water will enhance your connection with nature and dissolve all your stresses and worries away.

Enjoying your hot tub with your partner at night can be a whole new bathing experience and a very romantic one, too. The invigorating movement and warmth of the water is so powerful that it can help to energize and enhance a tired or struggling relationship. Other family members can enjoy a hot tub during the day, and bathing together really brings a family closer together.

HOW TO HAVE A LUXURIOUS BATHING EXPERIENCE

TRY THESE IDEAS TO MAKE THE MOST OF YOUR BATHROOM:

1	Set the mood and relax your face muscles and eyes with candles.
2	A scented bubble bath is sensual and fun.
3	Dead sea salts relax stiff muscles and soothe the soul.
4	Treat your feet with a pumice foot scrub.
5	Improve your circulation and treat cellulite with an exfoliating brush.
6	Give yourself a natural glow with a soft skin-polishing mitt.
7	Have a long soak until your worries dissolve away.
8	Heat a large thick towel for a sense of luxury and comfort.
9	Put on a silky robe and soft slippers.
10	Relax and do absolutely nothing.

Your imagination is the limit to creating a special bathing experience. Here a panoramic trompe l'oeil painting creates a view that didn't exist before.

SEE ALSO

THE HEALTHY HOME PAGE 14 —

FINDING YOUR STYLE PAGE 18 —

MOVING IN TOGETHER PAGE 26 —

LIGHT AND COLOR PAGE 150 —

bathing in light

WATER AND LIGHT. TWO OF THE ESSENTIAL FOUNDATIONS OF LIFE. BOTH INSTILL IN US A DEEP SENSE OF WELL-BEING. THIS ROOM COMBINES BOTH OF THESE FUNDAMENTALS IN A SPACE THAT BRIMS WITH POSITIVE ENERGY AND ATMOSPHERE.

BIG BATHTUB

If you have an ample supply of hot water, there is nothing more luxurious than a really big tub. They allow you to completely immerse yourself in water, rather than lie in a shallow trough as standard bathtubs force you to do. Big tubs also allow you to share the bathing experience.

As this titanic tub probably takes quite a while to fill, the owners have wisely installed a shower at one end for quick and easy washing.

SINKING FEELING

A tub this size is best sunk into the floor. It would dominate the room if it were standing on the floor and make the room feel cluttered and the bathers feel claustrophobic. The experience of sinking into a tub below floor level is a wonderfully energizing one. It enhances the inner cleansing process that is such a crucial part of bathing and leaves you feeling totally refreshed and ready for anything.

COLOR

Yellow is a perfect color for a sunny room. It is a happy, positive color that lifts the spirits and enhances the positive side of life. Here it is used in a tall room—the impact of the color all the stronger because of the expanse of wall that is used. When yellow is combined with sunlight, the combination is unbeatable as a cure for the blues. Anybody entering a sunlit yellow space like this will feel uplifted and energized. Yellow is also a good social color, in tune with the large bathtub for sharing.

WHITE MIRROR

By tiling the bottom part of the room in white, the designer has caused light to be reflected up into the ceiling, adding to the bright and uplifting effect. This also means that the entire floor is a wet area, allowing bathers the freedom to splash about. This will encourage a pleasurable, uninhibited bathing experience and enhance the fun aspects of your relationship. The shiny surface of the white tiles also contrasts well with the chalky texture of the yellow paint.

 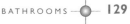
LIGHT

Two large windows guarantee that this is a room for bathing in light as well as water. The arrangement of windows with one on top of the other stops the high ceiling of the room from being a dark, cold, and unfriendly space. There is nothing more unsettling for bathers than to feel a negative, even threatening, space above them. In the evening, a simple sheer curtain offers privacy while the interior lights are on.

HEALING LIGHT

Light adds to the healing experience of bathing. It helps to elevate the experience of bathing from a purely physical, functional process to an emotionally and spiritually refreshing ritual. Bathing can be a very good time for reflection and thought—light means that your thoughts will be positive and creative. The effect on relationships is similar, since light helps us to look on the bright side.

BATH WITH A VIEW

There is something deeply rewarding about being able to lie in the comfort of your bathtub and gaze out of the window onto a pleasant view. Combining the very private activity of bathing with a view of the outside world is an enlivening experience. In this case, foliage brings another color into the room. It also suggests the goodness of nature, adding to the healing qualities of bathing.

SKY VIEW

Many people can't enjoy a view from their bathroom because they look out onto other houses or public areas. In these cases you could use a skylight to offer you an energizing view without having to worry about whose looking in. Lying in a tub with the lights off or turned down low and looking up at the stars is an experience to be savored.

feature tub

GIVEN CENTER STAGE, THIS TRADITIONAL WROUGHT-IRON TUB TURNS BATHING INTO A SPECIAL INDULGENCE, A RITUAL THAT DESERVES ABSOLUTE ATTENTION. THE FOCUS IS ENHANCED BY THE SIMPLE AND UNCLUTTERED DESIGN OF THE ROOM.

STARRING ROLE

Putting your bathtub in the middle of the room might seem like a mistake from the layout point of view. Actually, as long as the room is large enough, it can be the best place for it. After all, it is the principal object in the bathroom, so it deserves to be center stage. Other bathroom essentials such as the sink and toilet can be placed around the edge of the room. Bathing in the middle of the room is great for your self-confidence.

PLUMBING

It is best to get a plumber in to put in the water supply for your central bathtub. Fitting the taps on the side of the tub rather than at one end means you can share your bath easily and comfortably.

SPLASH OUT

If you are going to make a feature of your bathtub make it worthy of the attention. Traditional-style or antique baths have pleasing forms.

LIGHT

As in the previous page, this bathroom makes the most of the natural light that pours through a large window. In order to get a window that is big enough for the job, it is sometimes necessary to use a room that was not originally designed as a bathroom. Older homes that predate the fashion for large bathroom windows feature poor natural light resources. It might take some creative thinking to decide how you can get a bathroom with a good window—don't be afraid to try.

CANDLELIGHT

This bathroom is primed with candles, ready for a relaxing or romantic bath when night falls. Candlelight is particularly effective in the bathroom. The fire element directly opposes the water element, setting up a powerful set of extremes. The naked flame of a candle sparks creativity and passion, and a candlelit bathroom is the perfect setting for renewing the passion in a tired relationship. Dot small candles around the room for a magical, illuminating effect.

COLOR

A stark and traditional black and white floor sets the base tone for more subtle touches in the rest of the room. A very pale duck's-egg blue adds the essential touch of color to the room. This gentle color contains all the relaxing qualities of blue with some of the nurturing qualities of green. Cream-colored wood paneling eases the transition between the black and white floor and the blue walls, creating a neutral space for an added sense of calm.

REFLECTIONS

The wall color has been used to paint the outside of the bathtub. This creates a sense of cohesion within the room and prevents the tub from standing out too much. The effect is gentle on the eye and enhances the calming and restorative qualities of the room. The colors here are deeply sympathetic to relationships and will help to enhance communication and affection. Towels have been chosen to match the blue theme.

TRADITION WITH A TWIST

Traditional bathtub, black and white floor pattern, and wood paneling. All these things should make this room look extremely old-fashioned, even pompous. But with a few gentle touches, the traditional element is lifted and forms the basis for a welcoming, interesting bathroom. The most important modernizing element is the duck's-egg blue color theme discussed above. While it is not strikingly modern, it is nevertheless a self-assured color that contrasts with the rest of the room.

IN WITH THE NEW

Other touches keep the space from being purely traditional. A sculptural candelabra adds its elegant curves to the squares and straight lines of the room. A brightly colored picture contributes an irreverent touch of gaiety. All these things reflect a happy, confident relationship that is based on solid, traditional values, but is not afraid to explore new and different challenges together. A clearly personal bathroom such as this will help you understand your own relationship.

assess, discuss, and agree

IT IS A FINE BALANCING ACT TO MAKE YOUR BATHROOM A RELAXING AND COMFORTABLE RETREAT WHEN YOU MAY BE CONFINED BY SPACE AND THE POSSIBILITY OF SHARING WITH OTHER MEMBERS OF YOUR HOUSEHOLD. A GOOD PLACE TO START IS TO LOOK AT THE WAY YOU USE YOUR BATHROOM AND THINK ABOUT THE IMPROVEMENTS YOU WOULD LIKE TO MAKE. THIS MAKES DISCUSSING AND AGREEING ON CHANGES TO THE WAY YOU USE YOUR BATHROOM, ITS FACILITIES, AND ITS DECORATION MUCH EASIER.

First follow step one. Then exchange your answers with your partner so you can discover their real attitude to bathing and what they think about your existing bathroom. Find out who prefers to shower and who prefers to bathe, and whether your bathroom provides for both your needs. Discuss your attitude to bathing and how much privacy you get. You may be surprised by how much anxiety is caused by a cluttered, messy, and dreary bathroom. Once you have discussed these points, you can move to step two.

bathroom solutions

First discuss the points on which you agree and decide which improvements are possible in your bathroom, given the space and use. Remember that if you make large changes, you will need an alternative place to bathe while improvements are being carried out. If

step one

The first step is to discover how you view and use your bathroom. Read through the following statements and decide whether you agree or disagree with them. Then think about the facilities your ideal bathroom would have.

Many bathrooms have to suit a range of varying clientele, with very different ideas of what the bathroom is for. A well-planned bathroom takes everyone's needs into account and helps to maintain a smooth transition between the kids' splashing and Mom's relaxing evening soak.

check which use is appropriate to you:	PERSON A	PERSON B	PERSON C
Washing is purely functional, and I prefer to shower.			
I enjoy relaxing in the bathtub.			
The bathroom is used for children's bathing time.			
I find the bathroom is often being used when I need it.			
There is a lack of privacy in our bathroom.			
I would like to bathe with my partner.			
I find it hard to find time to relax and have a good soak.			
Our bathroom is messy and cluttered.			
My ideal bathroom would have			
a power jet shower			
a corner bathtub			
a spa bath			
a Jacuzzi			

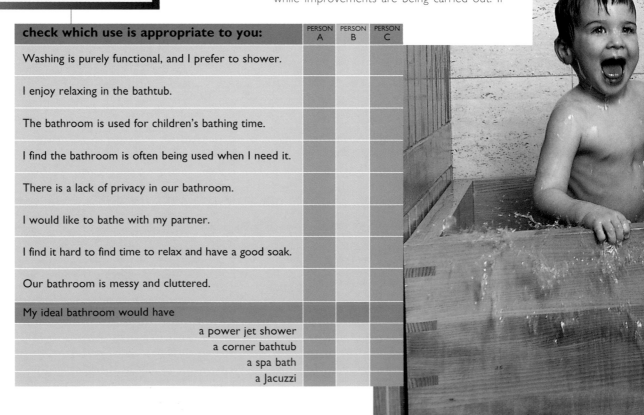

EXTRA HELP: STORAGE

Here is a checklist of all the things people often choose to store in the bathroom. Check the ones that apply to your place.

toothbrush and toothpaste
soaps and shower gels
shampoo and conditioner
hairbrush, comb, and hair products
medicines
household cleaning products
towels
robes
laundry basket
scales
wastebasket

Check to see whether you have a place for these items—not simply the edge of the bathtub or the sink. You will quickly see whether there are some things that do not have a home and the sort of extra storage you might need.

step two

The following questionnaire will help you identify the aspects of your bathroom that need improving.

you disagree on major points like what type of bathtub or shower to install, you should arrange a visit to some showrooms together so you can see all the alternatives. It could be that you end up changing your mind. Try to find a solution to your bathing needs by using lateral thinking. Perhaps you need to separate the bathtub and shower or incorporate extra bathing space in another room.

private luxury

Having a bathroom adjoining your bedroom is handy and provides you with privacy from the rest of the house.

Although there are many benefits to having a connecting bathroom, they have disadvantages. Steam and bad odors can leak out if the bathroom is not well ventilated, and noisy heaters and lights can disturb your partner when used at night. Sharing the same bathroom can be a nuisance, especially if you are a working couple who both need to get up at the same time. In this situation, double sinks and even a double shower are ideal.

tick which use is appropriate to you:	PERSON A	PERSON B	PERSON C
I think the bathroom fixtures need replacing.			
I think the shower needs improving.			
We need to improve the storage in the bathroom.			
The towels rods and heating need updating.			
The storage facilities need improving.			
We need to replace the mirror.			
The bathroom needs redecorating/re-tiling.			
The lighting needs improving.			
I think the bathroom needs total refurbishment and decoration.			

assess, discuss, and agree

BECAUSE THE BATHROOM IS SUCH A PRIVATE SPACE, SHARING IT WITH OTHERS CAN PROVE DIFFICULT. TO SHARE YOUR BATHROOM SUCCESSFULLY WITHOUT CONFLICT, IT MUST BE DESIGNED TO MAXIMIZE SPACE. YOU ALSO NEED TO ORGANIZE ITS USE TO REDUCE THE POSSIBILITY OF A RUSH HOUR JAM.

We often keep an amazing assortment of items in our bathrooms, so you can never have too much storage. If your bathroom is to be a clean, neat, and relaxing place, it is essential that it has a good selection of storage options. Incorporate different storage facilities like wall and floor cabinets with drawers, open shelves, hooks, or rods.

Everyone has their own bathing rituals and favorite bathing and toilet products, so keeping your bathroom clean and neat can be difficult, particularly if you share it with several people. One solution is to have enough storage facilities to give each person a cabinet, drawer or shelf space of their own. Individual laundry bags in different colors hanging on hooks will also minimize the accumulation of piles of dirty laundry. If your bathroom is too small for individualized storage space, then buy everyone a different-colored wash bag for each person's personal bathing and grooming items. To keep the bathroom free of clutter, everyone should keep their washbag, towel, and laundry in their bedroom.

Another key area is the allocation of bathroom time and the cleaning chores. There is nothing more stressful than a regular battle of the bathroom every morning. Chronic conflict such as this can put a serious strain on the relationships between homesharers. Use the following questionnaire and schedule maker to nip the problem in the bud and enjoy stress-free bathing.

Don't let the bathroom become a war zone. Keeping it neat and working out any timetable problems will help to reduce the risk of bathroom rage.

step one

The first step is to discover the extent of the bathroom-sharing problem, if there is one at all. All the homesharers should answer the following questions and then discuss the results. If there is a point of conflict, move on to step two.

	PERSON A	PERSON B	PERSON C
I need more personal storage space.			
I have to wait to use the bathroom.			
I don't use the bathroom at the time of day I would like to use it.			
I would like more time in the bathroom.			
There isn't enough hot water when I want to have a bath or shower.			
There aren't enough clean towels.			
We often run out of toilet paper.			
The bathroom is a mess.			
The bathroom is dirty.			
People forget to clean the bathtub/shower.			

step two

Try to resolve any points of conflict that come to light after step one through simple discussion. If any points remain, use the bathroom schedule maker below to portion out the precious bathroom time resources and to share the key chores.

If the amount of hot water available puts a limit on the number of baths or showers possible in a specific amount of time, factor this in to your schedule. For example, it may be that you can only allocate two baths for every morning and evening. It may be that more than one person needs to use the bathroom in the morning before going out to school or work. It is a good idea that the person who has to leave the earliest should use the bathroom first, but they also need to keep their time in the bathroom to a minimum since there are people waiting.

Try to cover all of these weekly tasks and time slots when completing your own bathroom schedule maker. If each person in the home is responsible for his own towels, soap, etc., ignore the relevant chores. The morning section of the table has been completed to demonstrate the system.

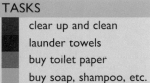

TIME SLOTS
- bathing time
- shower time
- quick wash

TASKS
- clear up and clean
- launder towels
- buy toilet paper
- buy soap, shampoo, etc.

MORNING

	MONDAY	TUESDAY	WEDNESDAY	THURSDAY	FRIDAY	SATURDAY	SUNDAY
6:00	person a	person b	person c	person d	person e	free	free
6:30	person b	person c	person d	person e	person f	person a	person b
7:00	person c	person d	person e	person f	person a	person b	person c
7:30	person d	person e	person f	person a	person f	person c	person d
8:00	person e	person f	person a	person b	person c	person d	person e
8:30	person f	person a	person b	person c	person d	person e	person f
9:00	free	free	free	free	free	person f	person a

EVENING

	MONDAY	TUESDAY	WEDNESDAY	THURSDAY	FRIDAY	SATURDAY	SUNDAY
6:30							
7:00							
7:30							
8:00							
8:30							
9:00							
9:30							
10:00							
10:30							

CHAPTER

6

into action

THIS CHAPTER WILL HELP YOU TO PLAN AND CARRY OUT THE DECORATING WORK ITSELF. THIS WILL INVOLVE DISCUSSING YOUR IDEAS, SETTING A BUDGET, SETTING UP A SCHEDULE OF WORKS, AND, WHERE NECESSARY, EMPLOYING A BUILDER OR TRADESPERSON. ACKNOWLEDGING YOUR INDIVIDUAL STRENGTHS AND WEAKNESSES WILL HELP YOU AGREE ON WHO DOES WHAT SO YOU CAN PUT YOUR PLANS INTO ACTION. BY WORKING THROUGH THIS CHAPTER, YOU WILL DISCOVER HOW TO WORK AS A TEAM TO OVERCOME CHALLENGES EFFECTIVELY AND THEN TO USE YOUR EXPERIENCE OF WORKING TOGETHER TO SOLVE OTHER PROBLEMS — AND IMPROVE YOUR RELATIONSHIP.

- ENTRANCE HALL
- LIVING ROOM
- KITCHEN
- BEDROOM
- BATHROOM

- DISCUSSION
- FOCUS
- INSPIRATION
- INTERACTION

getting started

ONCE YOU HAVE ASSESSED YOUR NEEDS AND AGREED ON THE CHANGES YOU ARE GOING TO MAKE, YOU NEED TO PUT YOUR PLANS INTO ACTION.

Even if you haven't done anything like this before, a decorating project can inspire you to develop a new skill and help you and your homesharers to work as a team. Home improvements do not always go smoothly, and you have to keep a positive outlook and a flexible frame of mind. Overcoming the obstacles and challenges as a couple or as a group can really strengthen your relationships so you can face and solve other problems in life with confidence.

who does what?

Deciding who does what depends on two things—time and skills. We all have different jobs to do, whether they are paid or unpaid. Acknowledging that you both have work and individual chores is a good starting point when deciding on how much time you can each contribute to your home project.

Sometimes one person is less able to participate in the decorating project due to demands of work or other commitments, but they may be able to take on the planning. This can make a major contribution to the

TOP TIPS FOR WORKING AS A TEAM

1 Express your feelings—when things aren't going well, discuss the problem before the job is completed.

2 Flexibility is strength—learning to cope with unforeseen circumstances and delays is an art that anyone can achieve.

3 Mutual support—when you support each other, it is much easier to find solutions to problems.

4 Stand together—a united front is essential when dealing with builders and suppliers.

5 Humor—try to see the funny side when things go wrong.

6 Encourage your partner—we all like praise when we have done a job well.

7 Take control—seeing your plans take form is empowering.

	SHOPPING AND ORDERING person A B C D	ACCOUNTANCY person A B C D	DRAWING PLANS person A B C D	PAINTING LARGE SURFACES person A B C D	PAINTING WOODWORK person A B C D	DECORATIVE EFFECTS person A B C D
I am good at						
I would like to try						
I think we should get a professional						

smooth running of the job. If your place only needs a good clean and clear up, it is not hard to find a couple of hours when you are both free. If you both work during the week and are going to share the practical tasks, the weekend may be the best time for carrying out the decorating—make sure you consult with neighbors if the work is likely to be noisy. Planning, organizing, ordering, and shopping is better done during the week using the phone or internet.

individual skills

Good working relationships are made by individuals pooling their skills and talents. So improving your home can give you an opportunity to show off your particular expertise as well as giving your partner the chance to impress you.

Trying out a decorating technique can be great fun, and you may find you have an undiscovered talent. Even if one person is more skillful than their partner, it is still worth doing the job together. Teaching and learning from your partner is a life skill that helps you communicate and brings you closer together.

The following table will help you work out the most suitable times to work together. It will also show, in a visual way, the balance of time you can contribute as individuals. Check the box when you have some time to spend on the project.

If you can devote planning and organization time— put O
If you can devote time to do practical tasks— put P

	DAY person A B C D	MORNING person A B C D	AFTERNOON person A B C D	EVENING person A B C D
monday				
tuesday				
wednesday				
thursday				
friday				
saturday				
sunday				

Discuss and decide on the days and times you can work together and the times you can contribute to the project when your partner may be busy.

WALLPAPERING person A B C D	TILING person A B C D	DIY/HANGING POLES/PUTTING UP SHELVES person A B C D	PLUMBING WORK person A B C D	MAKING FABRIC FURNISHINGS person A B C D	ELECTRICAL WORK person A B C D

starting work

WHEN IT COMES TO THE WORK ITSELF, YOU MAY BE SURPRISED AT HOW MUCH YOU CAN DO YOURSELVES. BUT DON'T TAKE ON MORE THAN YOU CAN MANAGE.

Painting and decorating does not require any specialized knowledge. You can do it successfully as long as you are well organized and have the right materials and equipment. You can usually get ladders, paints, brushes, and all the other tools you need under one roof in a hardware store or superstore.

painting

Most paint manufacturers produce small tester pots so you can try out a number of colors before committing to buying a large quantity. Look at the colors under different lighting conditions: tones can change dramatically in artificial light. Using a roller on the walls and

Techniques such as painting and wall-papering are easy to learn and are valuable skills to have at your disposal. There are plenty of "handy" courses around that will teach the basics. This should be enough to manage most of the jobs yourself, at a great financial saving.

Don't be afraid to take time over your choice of colors. Ending up with something you're unhappy with is much worse than not doing the work at all. Paint manufacturers print series of color swatches to help you.

0270-C

S

0505-B10G

S 0510-B10G

S 1010-B

S 0520-B10G

S 1020-B

S 0530-B10G

S 2020-B

S 0540-B10G

020-B

S 1040-B20G

0-B

ceilings makes painting quicker and easier, and you can usually paint the main areas in a room in just a few hours. One person should paint the large areas with a roller while the other uses a brush to get into the awkward areas. Painting woodwork takes longer, and you may find that one of you is better suited to this more exacting type of detail work.

wallpapering

Wallpapering is not as difficult as most people imagine. It is a task that is more successful when two people do it together. By dividing the task into different stages, you will soon work out your own system. After setting up your table and mixing your adhesive, you need to measure and cut each length of wallpaper. One person should apply the paste and then pass it on to their partner on a ladder. Depending on the length of the drop, this may entail folding the piece so it is easier to manage. If you both work at smoothing out the wallpaper with a sponge to get out any air bubbles, you will achieve a professional result.

getting in the builders

You will be able to do most decorating and unskilled jobs by yourselves by pooling your skills or trying out something new together. Invariably, there will be some things that are better left to experts. Choosing an architect, builder, or tradesperson is still part of your project and is something you should do together.

The best way to find a specialized tradesperson is through professional bodies and trade associations who require certain standards of skill. They should be able to recommend local firms and tradespeople.

Some jobs you can do yourself—but don't overestimate how much you can cope with.

Alternatively, you could ask your family, friends, and neighbors for recommendations. If your project requires building work, it may be wise to make sure your builder is insured and that they offer a guarantee.

Obtain three written quotes for each job before you decide to engage a builder. You also need to check their availability—the best contractors are often the busiest. Only accept the cheapest quote if you are confident the job will be done well. Often the middle quote is the better choice so as not to compromise quality.

Liaising with the builder is an important aspect of your project if you are to achieve a good result. Builders need encouragement but firmness. When problems occur, you should discuss and decide on your strategy before confronting the builder so you do not give out conflicting instructions.

planning and organization

WHEN YOU HAVE DECIDED TO DO YOUR HOME IMPROVEMENTS, YOU NEED TO SCHEDULE A TIME TO GET STARTED. IN ORDER TO MINIMIZE DISRUPTION TO YOUR HOME LIFE AND WORK SCHEDULE (AND TO AVOID CONFLICT), YOU NEED TO PLAN THE SEQUENCE OF EVENTS CAREFULLY.

Without planning, home improvements can become a nightmare. You need to make a list of the changes you wish to make and any new furniture and fixtures you may need. This will help you set a budget. Finances can put a huge strain on relationships and turn an exciting project into a depressing one. So it is important to have a clear idea about your financial limits at the outset. Doing the work yourself will save money, but you also need to budget for specialized work.

plan and organize

If you have decided to do major improvements to your place, you need to minimize disruption to your home by

WHICH SKILLS YOU HAVE AND HOW TO USE THEM

When deciding who does what, bear in mind that:

1 A good telephone manner is good for ordering and chasing deliveries.

2 Computer literacy will enable you to source and buy goods via the internet.

3 Accounting skills are useful for setting a budget and comparing the costs of different items.

4 Measuring accurately is an essential skill for purchasing furniture and furnishings for your home.

5 Drawing skills are handy for plans and furniture layouts.

6 Good visual skills help with choice of colors and combinations for decorating and textiles.

	entrance	living room
week one		
week two		
week three		
week four		

arranging to do one room at a time. Sometimes it is more cost- and time-effective to do all the plumbing or electrical work at the same time, which could leave you without power and water. So make sure you know when utilities will be disconnected or try to make sure you still have light and water somewhere else in the house. Making a weekly planner is essential for bigger projects since it helps you keep an eye on your schedule even if it has to change as you go along. Decide which room should be

kitchen	dining room	bedroom	bathroom

SEVEN STEPS TO HOME HEAVEN

1 plan and organize

2 shop and order goods

3 hire contractors / do the work yourselves

4 purchase individual items of furniture and lighting

5 purchase all your curtains and fabric furnishings

6 arrange your room and put in the finishing touches

7 celebrate

decorated first and then allocate a suitable period of time to each space in your home. If you are using a builder or other tradesmen, ask them to estimate the length of time it will take for them to complete the job. Remember that decorating and building work always takes longer than you anticipate, so add some extra time to your initial estimate.

ordering and shopping

Rather than lumping all purchasing and shopping together, it is a good idea to separate the practical from the decorative. Finding everything you need can take time, and you may have to use computer, accounting and phone skills. Although one partner may have more time than the other to devote to shopping, there are many preparations, such as measuring, that also have to be done. Shopping for furniture and decorative items can be fun and should be something you do together.

furniture, fittings, and finishing touches

ONCE THE BUILDING AND DECORATION WORK IS COMPLETE, YOU WILL HAVE TO THINK ABOUT THE NEW FURNITURE AND FIXTURES. THESE DAYS, THERE IS A HUGE CHOICE OF FURNITURE. YOU CAN BUY NEW OR OLD, FLATPACKED OR CUSTOM-MADE. IT TAKES A CERTAIN FLAIR TO BE ABLE TO MIX DIFFERENT STYLES OF FURNITURE IN A ROOM. UNLESS YOU ARE CONFIDENT, IT IS BEST TO LIMIT YOURSELF TO NO MORE THAN THREE DIFFERENT TYPES IF YOU WANT YOUR HOME TO HAVE CONTINUITY AND NOT RESEMBLE A JUNK SHOP.

In many areas of your home, you may need to put in furniture that comes flatpacked. Assembling the pieces on your own can be difficult; working as a team can make all the difference. First, make sure you have all the contents. One person should then read out the instructions while the other checks the contents, so you get it right first time.

antiques and collectables

In your home you will undoubtedly want individual pieces of furniture and special items. If you are looking for antiques or collectables, you may need to travel to a market or auction house with a good selection. Searching through specialized magazines and attending garage sales can make shopping for these items a special experience in itself. Finding something unique that you really like always creates a good feeling in your home.

fabric furnishings

Fabric furnishings give a room its finishing touches, so they are best left until last. When you have finished the walls and have installed the floor covering, you will be better able to coordinate your curtains, blinds, and other fabric furnishings.

Your place may be near a big furniture warehouse or furniture stores, but if you don't want the hassle of chain-store shops, you can always shop by mail order. The disadvantage with this when buying furniture is that you cannot actually sit on the sofa or lie on the bed, so you need to make sure the company offers you a full refund policy.

CAREFUL COMBINATIONS

Combine no more than three of the following in any one room:

1 modern furniture in light wood or wood veneer

2 built-in or integrated units, in wood, glass, metal, or laminate

3 traditional or period furniture in dark wood with inlay or carving

4 global lifestyle theme in wood, cane, bamboo, or metal

5 furniture incorporating granite, marble, ceramic, or stone

6 furniture made from metal, molded plastic, glass, or other rigid materials

7 French country or Shaker-style furniture in natural wood, color-washed or painted

Shopping for furnishings and fabrics from catalogs can be difficult, and it is far better to do this in person. Pictures in catalogs are never a perfect color match, nor can you feel the texture or weight of a fabric. Always get samples sent to you before purchasing by mail order. If you are unable to go looking for furnishings, you could employ an interior decorator who will help you coordinate your decor and bring suitable sample fabrics to your home. A cheaper option is to go into a local furnishing shop and look through their sample books.

Once you have chosen a selection of fabrics from a sample book, catalog or store, it is best to borrow or buy a full-length sample so you can see the effect in situ. Take turns to hold up the different lengths of fabric alongside the window so you can really see how it will look. This will also help you decide which colors and patterns work well together and will match your color scheme.

If you have sewing and upholstery skills, you may decide to make some of the curtains and furnishing items yourself. Use your creativity to choose a style that is in keeping with the style and atmosphere you want to create in your home.

finishing touches

Your home grows and changes with you, so it is never really complete. The most precious items in our homes often come by accident. They may be a gift or something you find unexpectedly. So don't rush shopping for finishing touches—your home will evolve naturally and reflect your changing life.

time to celebrate

Completing your home improvement project calls for a celebration. When you clear up clutter or redecorate, you are symbolically cleaning out the old and inviting in the new. The look and atmosphere in your newly decorated room may seem unfamiliar at first, so you need to make friends with the new space. Celebrating your success gives you the opportunity to show off your new look to your friends and family. When your place is filled with laughter and positive thoughts, the room will absorb the happy atmosphere, offering you support in times to come.

Fabric furnishings should be chosen to fit around the style that you have chosen for the rest of the decoration project. In some cases you may have a particular fabric in mind that inspires the whole look of the scheme.

CHAPTER

7

creating atmosphere

IN THIS CHAPTER, YOU WILL FIND DETAILS OF DIFFERENT TECHNIQUES YOU CAN USE TO MAKE YOUR ROOMS

REALLY WORK AND FEEL RIGHT. THE SUBTLE VIBRATIONS EXERTED BY LIGHT, COLOR, AROMA, AND SOUND

CAN BE VITAL IN CREATING A HARMONIOUS ATMOSPHERE IN YOUR HOME. FENG SHUI UTILISES THESE COSMIC

FORCES TO HELP YOU BALANCE ENERGY IN YOUR PLACE, SO YOU CAN ENJOY VITALITY AND GOOD HEALTH.

BY MAKING YOUR HOME FULL OF POSITIVE ENERGY, IT WILL HELP YOU DEVELOP AND MAINTAIN A LOVING

ATTITUDE TOWARD YOURSELF, YOUR PARTNER, AND YOUR HOMESHARERS.

the art of feng shui

FENG SHUI IS PRONOUNCED "FUNG SHWAY" AND LITERALLY TRANSLATED MEANS "WIND AND WATER." IT IS A SUBTLE FORM OF INTERIOR DESIGN THAT BALANCES AND ENHANCES THE ENERGIES AROUND YOU.

This ancient art is based on the idea that when we live in harmony with nature we will enjoy good luck and prosperity. The central principle of feng shui is the concept of the life-giving force or energy called chi. When chi flows unrestricted through our homes and bodies, we connect to the universal forces around us and thus experience harmony and good health.

The main aim of feng shui is to moderate and enhance the flow of chi around our environment, so promoting a good supply of life energy. By clearing clutter and moving furniture, you create a clear path for the energizing chi to move around your home.

Like fresh, clean air, chi should move freely through all the rooms in your home. Chi can easily get blocked in dark corners, rooms that are closed up, under stairs, and under furniture. When you remove clutter and open up the room so light and air can enter, you will immediately enhance the atmosphere. Light and sound are powerful forces that can move stagnant energy. By hanging a wind chime or mobile in a narrow doorway or dark passage, you will breathe new energy into the atmosphere. Crystal pendants hung in windows are another feng shui cure that stimulates the movement of chi and helps create a positive atmosphere in a room.

In addition to flowing around the bedroom, chi should also be able to flow under the bed. This encourages fresh energy to reach you as you sleep, helping you to wake feeling refreshed and revived.

ENHANCING CHI

By using the principles of feng shui it is possible to improve any environment. A supportive home will improve your relationships, your finances, health, and career. Each part of your life is linked to a compass direction and that area of the home.
By enhancing the flow of chi in that area of your home, you can improve the corresponding area in your life.

1 South governs recognition and fame.

2 Southwest governs marriage and marital happiness.

3 West governs children.

4 Northwest governs helpful people and mentors.

5 North governs career prospects.

6 Northeast governs education.

7 East governs family relationships and health.

The hall is the principal place where chi enters the home. While it should be able to flow easily into the rest of the home, the flow shouldn't be too direct and brutal.

A healthy flow of chi is most important in rooms where you spend a lot of time. An arrangement around a central point is the ideal for the living room.

STIMULATE YOUR CHI

Feng shui cures to improve the flow of chi:

1 Clear away clutter from the floor and tabletops to allow chi to circulate.

2 Remove big or dark furniture from a room that makes a heavy, depressing atmosphere.

3 Hang a wind chime at your front or back door to bring more healthy energy into your home.

4 Plants in a room promote good chi and cleanse electronic smog from electrical equipment.

5 A crystal pendant in a window can clear the air in an unused or dark room.

A good chi flow helps the bathroom remain fresh and enhances its restorative qualities.

IMPROVING YOUR RELATIONSHIPS WITH FENG SHUI

The area of your home that governs the energy in your relationships is the southwest corner. Making sure that you have good feng shui in this part of your home will enhance your relationships and attract romance.

1 Natural quartz crystals placed in the southwestern corner will activate your marriage area, as will a photo of you as a couple in the southwestern area of your living room or bedroom.

2 Place symbols of romance in pairs in the relationship corner — ornaments of mandarin ducks, paintings of peonies, or silk flowers are very auspicious.

3 Place family mementoes in the eastern corner to enhance family relationships.

4 Enhance relationships with your children by placing photos or other objects relating to them in the western part of your home.

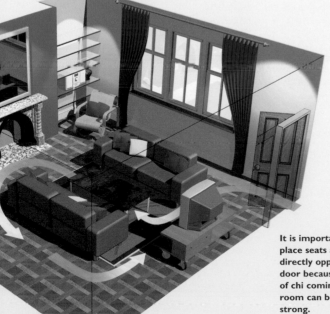

It is important not to place seats and sofas directly opposite the door because the flow of chi coming into the room can be too strong.

The creative center that is the kitchen needs a good supply of chi to remain positive and plentiful.

light and color

THE AMOUNT OF LIGHT THAT COMES INTO YOUR HOME CAN PLAY A SIGNIFICANT PART IN CREATING A HEALTHY AND JOYFUL ATMOSPHERE. LIGHT AFFECTS BOTH OUR BIOLOGICAL AND PHYSIOLOGICAL HEALTH, AND WHEN WE LIVE IN A BRIGHT AND LIGHT ENVIRONMENT, WE HAVE PLENTY OF ENERGY AND GLOW WITH GOOD HEALTH. INSURING A GOOD SUPPLY OF NATURAL LIGHT IS CRUCIAL FOR CREATING A HEALTHY HOME.

We all need all the colors of the spectrum—as seen in rainbows—to remain healthy and happy. Your home should bring you plenty of light and color.

In order to be healthy, we need exposure to the light waves found in sunlight. If we do not receive at least 30 minutes of natural sunlight every day, we can suffer from many mental, emotional, and physical problems. Deficiency of natural light has been identified as an illness known as Seasonal Affective Disorder or SAD, with symptoms that range from nervous fatigue and eyestrain to lowered immune system and, possibly, depression and poor sleep patterns. If you suffer from any of these problems, especially during the winter months, you should try to increase the amount of natural sunlight in your home and life.

Most people spend a great deal of time living with artificial light. Lengthy exposure to any one type of light can leave you feeling sluggish or tired, so it is important to introduce as wide a range of lights as possible

OUR RESPONSES TO COLORS

Understanding the qualities and effect of different colors on you will help you select colors for your home that will reflect and support you as individuals and as a couple.

Red is warming and stimulating.

Orange is cheerful and uplifting.

Yellow is friendly and sunny.

Brown/copper is warm, nurturing, and earthy.

Green is soothing and relaxing.

Blue is calming and quieting.

Purple is inspirational and dramatic.

Pink/peach/apricot is gentle and supportive.

HOME LIGHT THERAPY

Everyone feels the immediate benefits of being in a light and airy environment. Try these ideas to increase the amount of light in your life:

1   Spend at least 30 minutes a day in your yard or going for a walk.

2   Bring more daylight into your home by opening a window.

3   Keep all your windows super clean inside and out.

4   Tie or pull back your curtains from the window.

5   Use light-filtering fabrics for shades and curtains.

6   Make sure you have several different types of light in every room.

7   Use full-spectrum light bulbs in your lamps during winter months.

SEVEN USEFUL PRINCIPLES OF USING COLOR

1   Light colors are easier to live with.

2   Rich strong colors force a specific mood on the room.

3   Dark colors are good for accents and quickly change the atmosphere in a room.

4   Combine warm and cool colors in a room to create variety and balance.

5   In private spaces, use colors that express your personality, style, and personal needs.

6   In shared spaces, use neutrals if you want to combine several strong colors.

7   When using tones of one color, incorporate texture for sensory stimulation.

QUICK WAYS TO BRING COLOR INTO A ROOM

Color is the simplest way to give your home a new look. The effect is immediate, and the cost isn't huge.

1 A bright table runner or tablecloth creates an atmosphere of home comfort.

2 A bunch of bright flowers gives a room an immediate lift.

3 A colorful and aromatic potted plant brings long-lasting seasonal color.

4 An arrangement of red and yellow candles energizes a room.

5 A bowl of oranges or lemons brings focus to the mind.

6 Colored-paper lanterns create a party atmosphere.

7 A row of contrasting scatter cushions can hide a tired sofa.

8 A rich-toned rug pulls a cold room together.

9 A collection of framed greeting cards creates a talking point.

10 A colorful throw will make an old chair look more comfortable.

11 Colored glass bottles on a windowsill are inspirational.

into your home. During winter months, it is worth investing in some full-spectrum light bulbs for your lamps. These have the same proportions of colors as normal sunlight and can radically improve symptoms of SAD.

During the short days of winter, you can also introduce other forms of natural light into your home. Candles and firelight are easy on the eye and also bring a feeling of warmth and love into your home.

color therapy

Color therapy is both an ancient art and a modern scientific tool. It recognizes that color is a dynamic energy that can be used as an agent of support and force for change to the routine stresses of daily life.

Color is the first and most important means of creating a relaxed and harmonious atmosphere around you. Not only are your spirits lifted, but your body will function better, too. Each color vibration has its own qualities and action upon us, although we may respond to colors in an individual way. Being surrounded by colors that make you feel comfortable and happy put you in the right frame of mind for building healthy relationships. While your favorite colors will make you feel confident and happy, specific colors can have life-enhancing qualities, too. Certain colors improve your pulse rate, heart beat, blood pressure, and nervous and muscular tension so you are better able to deal with stress.

SEE ALSO

OUR HOMES, OURSELVES PAGE 10

CHOOSING COLOR PAGE 22

MOVING IN TOGETHER PAGE 26

SHARING A HOME PAGE 28

aromatherapy

THE ART OF AROMATHERAPY IS A VERY ANCIENT ONE. TODAY ESSENTIAL OILS AND NATURAL SCENTS ARE STILL USED FOR THEIR HEALING AND MOOD-ENHANCING PROPERTIES. SOME OILS HAVE STRONG DISINFECTING PROPERTIES, WHILE OTHERS ARE MOOD ENHANCING. YOU CAN USE AROMATHERAPY IN MANY WAYS TO HELP YOU CREATE A SUPPORTIVE AND PROTECTIVE HOME ENVIRONMENT.

entrances

The aroma in your entrance hall will be unique because this is where the aromas from all parts of your home mingle. The scent of a happy home will be very different from an unhappy one, so it is important that the scents permeating your place are pleasant and attractive. A few drops of essential oil on a doormat gives a special welcome.

living room

The living room is the main area that collects many different aromas both from the furnishings and from people. These conflicting scents create a whirlpool, each one clashing with another. In order to create a harmonious environment where you can relax and enjoy yourself, you need to cleanse these conflicting aromas and instill a new and coordinated mix of scents. To clear the old vibrations out, clean and air the room thoroughly and then use essential oils to create the type of atmosphere you want.

kitchens and eating places

The kitchen is the place with which we most associate household smells. The wonderful mixture of natural aromas from fruits, vegetables, and herbs can make the kitchen a welcoming and seductive place, but unfortunately kitchens are also the source of many unwanted and harmful smells.

Many household cleaners are scented with artificial aromas to which many people are allergic. These sprays not only give your kitchen a clinical aroma, but can cause such

ENERGIZING AND STIMULATING	WARM AND SECURE	REFRESHING AND UPLIFTING	MENTAL AND MEMORY STIMULANT	CLEANSING AND PURIFYING
living room, dining room playroom, games or fitness room, stairs	small living room bedroom	living room, study kitchen, workroom	study, work area	kitchen, utility room relaxation area
ginger, rosemary, peppermint, lavender, cinnamon, clary sage	chamomile, ylang ylang, clary sage, tangerine, lavender	sandalwood, lemon, rosemary,	basil, lemongrass, cardamon, grapefruit, camphor, patchouli, peppermint	tea-tree, lavender, thyme, juniper, eucalyptus, rosemary, lime, pine

problems as asthma, headaches, skin rashes, and nausea. Aromatic herbs and oils can make effective and environmentally friendly alternatives to many chemical air fresheners.

bedroom

There are many ways to enjoy aroma in your bedroom. A drop of essential oil on a pillow can help you to relax as you drift off to sleep, while an incense stick will help you calm the mind. Scented sachets and lining papers will give your clothing a fresh or sensual aroma and aromatic candles will instill your bedroom with loving and healing vibrations.

bathroom

Like the kitchen, the bathroom should not smell like a lemon tree or pine forest long after you have cleaned it. If you want to make your bathing sanctuary a place where you can release the tension of the day, you should choose cleaning products with light natural fragrances. Place a couple of drops of essential oil on the cardboard inside a roll of toilet paper to soak up the aroma and release it gradually over a period of time. You can also use a bowl containing potpourri as a colorful and healthy way of keeping your

bathroom smelling fresh and clean. The bathroom provides the perfect setting for an extended aromatherapy session. Scented candles release tension in the eyes and face, and aromatic oils can be either stimulating, detoxifyng or relaxing. There are many natural beauty products such as body lotions, face, and hand creams that contain essential oils and that will bring out your natural beauty. Essential oils are strong, so read the labels carefully before using them.

QUICK GUIDE TO AROMAS	
1	Floral scents are warming, secure and romantic.
2	Citrus aromas are refreshing, cleansing and invigorating.
3	Herby scents are appetizing, purifying and uplifting.
4	Woody aromas deter insects and create a feeling of protection.
5	Spicy scents are energizing, stimulating and warming.
6	Exotic aromas are sensual, relaxing and comforting.

CALMING AND RELAXING	BALANCING AND RESTORING	INSECT DETERRENTS	ROMANTIC	PROTECTION
bedroom, bathroom quiet room	living room, bedroom quiet area	in all rooms, patio drawers, cupboards	bedroom, living room bathroom	all the home where needed, yoga, relaxation or meditation area.
sandalwood, chamomile, geranium, rose otto, ylang ylang, orange, marjoram	neroli, geranium, rose, cypress, lemon	lavender, citronella, peppermint, lemongrass, thyme, basil, cinnamon	ylang ylang, jasmine, rose, geranium, sandalwood	sandalwood, frankincense, lavender, cedar wood

sound therapy

SOUND IS PROBABLY ONE OF THE MOST IGNORED AREAS OF INTERIOR DECORATION. ALTHOUGH IT CANNOT BE SEEN, IT HAS A GREAT EFFECT ON YOUR ENJOYMENT OF YOUR HOME. IT HAS BEEN KNOWN FOR THOUSANDS OF YEARS THAT MUSIC CAN RELIEVE STRESS, AND TODAY SOUND THERAPY IS FREQUENTLY USED FOR ITS RELAXING PROPERTIES IN STORES, HOTELS, AND AIRPORTS AROUND THE WORLD.

In the modern world, we are continually bombarded with high-volume sound vibrations, and even in our homes we do not escape from sound pollution. Exposure to negative vibrations sustained over a long period of time can eventually cause the body to deviate from its natural resonance, resulting in stress and possible ill health.

Scientists have confirmed that sound affects our blood circulation, nervous system, metabolism, and the workings of our endocrine glands. Sounds that are in tune with our body rhythms promote and maintain our health, while those that do not synchronize with us can cause illness. So it is important to block out harmful sounds as well as to introduce healing ones into your home. To minimize noise from outside, insulate your floors, walls, and ceilings if your home is located in a shared building. Double and triple glazing will radically deaden external sounds.

Every material you have in the home has its own sound quality. Walking on different materials also produces different sounds which will vary with your footwear. If you walk on wood, stone, or tiles it will create soft, muffled tones, while carpet deadens sound altogether. These subtle noises can have strong subconscious effects on our mood and emotions. Gravel and doormats create sounds that let the inhabitants know that there is someone entering the home.

music in your home

The human body and spirit respond so well to musical vibrations that people who surround themselves with melodious music are often much happier, calmer, and relaxed than those who do not have music in their lives. Music has a direct effect on our emotions, bypassing our mental faculties so we respond immediately and intuitively to the rhythms and melodies. Music comes directly from the heart, and with music we can touch someone's heart in the same direct and loving way.

The messages and feelings sent out by the musical rhythms have an instant and subconscious effect on us. Some music will have a good effect on us and other music a bad one. Music made up of discordant, jarring sounds and broken rhythms promotes an atmosphere of anger, aggression, and discord. It is out of synch with our natural rhythms and really can have a bad influence on our mind and influence our behavior. When you fill your home with beautiful music, you naturally relax and become more open and receptive to your partner.

Music and sound have powerful effects on our emotions. They can be used to create a specific mood in a room, working with your color and lighting scheme. Music can also be used to transport you to a place far away from the here and now.

SEVEN WAYS TO BRING HEALING SOUNDS INTO YOUR HOME.

1 Fit a soft chiming front door bell that makes harmonious notes.

2 Install an old-fashioned door bell on a pulley.

3 Find a special door knocker.

4 Use a stereo with a timer that will play natural sounds to wake you up.

5 Hang musical chimes made of wood, bamboo, shells, ceramics, glass, or metal.

6 Introduce a water feature using running water into your home.

7 Hang feeders at windows to attract wild birds.

There are many ways you can use sound in the home to make you feel relaxed and stress free. If you love music, incorporate an integral sound system into your home improvement design. Decide where you wish to hear music and install wiring and speaker outlets with other electrical work to carry music throughout your place.

index

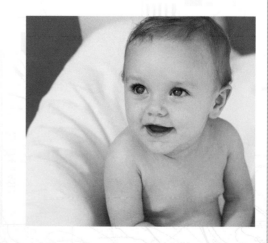

USEFUL ADDRESSES

Feng Shui

Feng Shui Society
18 Alacross Road
London W5 4HT, UK
Tel: (020) 8567 2043

The Feng Shui Institute of America
PO Box 488
Wabasso
FL 32970, USA
Tel: (0407) 589 9900

Holistic Design Institute
Farfields House
Jubilee Road, Totnes, Devon
TQ9 5BP, UK
Tel: (01803) 868 037
www.holisticdesign.co.uk

Color and Light

International Association of Color
46 Cottenham Road
Histon
Cambridge
CB4 9ES, UK
Tel: (01223) 563403

The Institute for Light Energy Research
449 Santa Fe Drive, Ste. 246
Encinitas, CA 92024, USA
Tel: (0619) 944 2934

Iris International School of Colour Therapy
Farfields House
Jubilee Road
Totnes, Devon, UK
Tel: (01803) 868037
www.iriscolour.co.uk

Aromatherapy and Sound

American Music Therapy Association
8455 Colesville Road, Suite 1000
Silver Spring, Maryland 20910, USA
Tel: (0301) 589 3300
info@musictherapy.org

IFA – International Federation of Aromatherapists
182 Chiswick High Road
London W4 1PP, UK
Tel: (020) 8742 2605
www.int-fed-aromatherapy.co.uk

picture credits

Many thanks to the following for supplying pictures for this book:

Elizabeth Whiting Associates:
pages 1, 2, 4, 8, 9, 14, 12, 20, 30, 31, 32, 34, 36, 38, 39, 42, 44, 46, 49, 50, 51, 56, 58, 62, 66, 68, 70, 72, 76, 77, 78, 82, 84, 88, 92, 98, 99, 103, 104, 106, 108, 110, 112, 114, 118, 119, 120, 126, 128, 132.

Robert Harding:
pages 2, 94, 118, 130.

acknowledgments

Many thanks to the following for their help with this book:

Amy's Limited,

Hertfordshire, United Kingdom

Amazing Grates,

London, United Kingdom

Broadway Pet Stores,

London, United Kingdom

Jennie Mann Florists,

London, United Kingdom

The Pier,

London, United Kingdom

Magnet

Enfield, United Kingdom

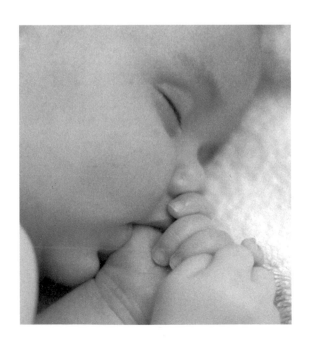